FRANCE

Benjamin Péret

TWAS 359

Radovan Ivsic

Benjamin Péret

Benjamin Péret

By J. H. MATTHEWS

Syracuse University

TWAYNE PUBLISHERS

A DIVISION OF G. K. HALL & CO., BOSTON

Library of Congress Cataloging in Publication Data

Matthews, J H
    Benjamin Péret.

    (Twayne's world authors series ; TWAS 359 : France)
    Bibliography: pp. 169-72
    Includes index.
    1. Péret, Benjamin, 1899–1959—Criticism and Inter-
pretation.
PQ2631.E348Z7   841'.912   74-30229
ISBN 0–8057–2691–8

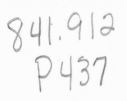

For E. F. Granell

A bon entendeur salut

Contents

About the Author

J. H. Matthews is Professor of French at Syracuse University. Since 1965 he has been editor of *Symposium: A Quarterly Journal in Modern Foreign Literatures.* He is editor of a selection of stories by Guy de Maupassant (1959) as well as of two special issues of *La Revue des Lettres Modernes*, and author of *Les deux Zola* (1957) and numerous articles on nineteenth- and twentieth-century literature. His interest in surrealism had led him to write also *An Introduction to Surrealism* (1965), *An Anthology of French Surrealist Poetry* (1966), *Surrealism and the Novel* (1966), *André Breton* (1967), *Surrealism Poetry in France* (1969), *Surrealism and Film* (1971), *Theatre in Dada and Surrealism* (1974), and *The Custom-House of Desire: a half-century of surrealist stories* (1975). His *Péret's Score / Vingt poèmes de Benjamin Péret* appeared in 1965, illustrated by the Surrealist painter E. F. Granell. He is a founder member of the Association of the Friends of Benjamin Péret.

Preface

It is safe to say that of all the writers represented in Twayne's World Authors Series none is quite so out of place as Benjamin Péret, in a survey of the world's literature. It is not that Péret is to be judged an inferior performer in his chosen medium, and therefore undeserving of the attention that, paradoxically, readers are being asked to give him here. Rather, his writings confront us with a difficulty that relates directly to his unique gifts.

Péret's work vigorously resists classification as literature, and can be understood and enjoyed fully only by those who bear this in mind or, better still, are not confined in their response within the limitations of literary practice. In prose and verse, Péret's texts display their originality in a form of poetry that takes definition from violent opposition to the idea that a poem is a mode of literary expression. Hence, as the first book in English on Benjamin Péret, the present study has two distinct but related aims.

Virtually unknown to the general public, in France or anywhere else, Benjamin Péret made a contribution to Surrealism that, within the Surrealist movement, is acknowledged to be irreplaceable. Not long before Péret's death in September, 1959, André Pieyre de Mandiargues asserted in the *Nouvelle Revue Française* (February, 1959), "No one else can now or in the future presume to represent surrealist poetry fully and purely." Other French Surrealists, better known than Péret and far more widely respected outside the Surrealist circle, have testified eloquently to the reputation he enjoyed among his peers. Louis Aragon wrote in *Commerce* (Autumn, 1924) that Benjamin Péret was "a great poet such as they don't make any more." "*I*," declared Philippe Soupault in an article published in *Arts* in 1963, "would give all of the work of Eluard for a single poem by Péret." As for the leader of Surrealist activities in France, André

Breton, he remarked of Péret as early as 1922, in the course of a public lecture delivered in Barcelona, "He is, I don't conceal the fact, one of the men I experience the most emotion from knowing." In "Towards a Third Manifesto of Surrealism," published in *New Directions* in 1940, Nicolas Calas was to assert, "A force of purer quality than the one the poetry of Péret possesses does not exist in or outside surrealism." For French Surrealists of a later generation, Gérard Legrand, who joined the movement in 1948, is a representative spokesman. The month Péret died, Legrand wrote in *Arts*, "At the age when one sees mountebanks and 'cheats' increasing in number, he appeared to me as *a man all of a piece*. What a marvelous certainty: to know that this man is possible, to look at him." Younger still, Pierre Dhainaut, insisting in *Symposium* (Winter, 1966) upon the "capital role played by Péret in the surrealist adventure," has spoken of Péret's work as "one of the most exemplary that surrealism has offered."

In spite of all this, the work of Péret is generally ignored, or treated with indifference and insensitivity, not to say hostility, by those, writing in France and abroad, who devote themselves to the study of Surrealism. And so one of the purposes underlying this examination of Péret's contribution to Surrealism is to acquaint readers who do not yet know them with the richness of Péret's writings. The other aim is to consider why his work has not been granted the attention it deserves, even by those who aspire to an objective assessment of Surrealism.

The problem for those whose training has prepared them to conduct analyses of works of literature is that the characteristic elements of Péret's writing, dictated by his conception of poetry, elude classification under the rubric of literary style. They do this so successfully that the literary commentator, aware above all of the absence of poetry as he has learned to recognize it, may feel within his rights in condemning the writings of Péret as antipoetic. For this reason, the second aim of this study is not pursued in a spirit of partisanship, but with the intention of defining poetry as Benjamin Péret practiced it with a dedication that made him the envy of his contemporaries in Surrealism and the object of admiration among younger participants in the Surrealist venture. And for this reason, too, a rehearsal of views ex-

Preface

pressed by critics on both sides of the Atlantic is less to our purpose than taking into account the comments elicited by Péret's work from within the Surrealist movement.

Benjamin Péret's work, Dhainaut has pointed out, "embodies, all by itself one might say without risk of exaggeration, surrealist poetry founded on automatism, on the resources of the image, creative of myths, revealing desire, spreading the marvelous through words, through things, everywhere." Since the word "marvelous" takes on special color in Surrealism, particularly as used by Péret, the two aims that give direction to the present study can best be brought into focus if we ask the following questions. What did the marvelous mean to Benjamin Péret? How can his understanding of the marvelous, and of the part to be played by automatism in attaining the marvelous, be said to provide a key to Péret's poetic universe and to his view of the poet as a revolutionary forever opposed to society? In seeking answers to these questions, we can hope to discover why the American Surrealist Franklin Rosemont, who so enthusiastically praises Péret's "admirably incurable passion for all that is marvelous," has asserted in *Radical America* (August, 1970) that for some people like himself, Benjamin Péret is "one of the surest guides of the spirit through the labyrinth of contemporary confusion."

Two chapters of this book expand upon material previously published under the titles noted below. Reproduction of the material in question is by kind permission of the journals cited: "Mechanics of the Marvellous: the short stories of Benjamin Péret," *L'Esprit créateur*; "Invective et Merveilleux dans *Je ne mange pas de ce pain-là* de Benjamin Péret," *Kentucky Romance Quarterly*. Another section elaborates upon an essay entitled "Benjamin Péret: Marvelous Conjunction" in Mary Ann Caws, ed., *Text and Theory*, Wayne State University Press, 1974, and appears by permission of the publisher. Special thanks are due Jehan Mayoux, who made available rare and unpublished documents.

J. H. MATTHEWS

Syracuse University

Chronology

1899 Born in Rézé, near Nantes.

1917– Military service, for which he volunteers to please his
1919 mother, who raised him and his brother after her separa-
tion from their father in 1901.

1920– Participation in the Dada movement.
1922

1921 Publication of *Le Passager du transatlantique.*

1923 Publication of *Au 125 du boulevard Saint-Germain.*

1924 Publication of *Immortelle Maladie.*

1924– Coeditor of *La Révolution surréaliste.*
1925

1925 Publication of *Il était une boulangère* and (in collaboration with Paul Eluard) of *152 Proverbes mis au goût du
jour.*

1927 Joins the Communist Party and works for a while on the
Communist newspaper *L'Humanité.* Marries the Brazilian
singer Elsie Houston. Publication of *Dormir, dormir dans
les pierres* and (in collaboration with Louis Aragon,
André Breton, Paul Eluard, and Pierre Unik) of *Au
Grand Jour.*

1928 Publication of . . . *Et les Seins mouraient* . . . and *Le
Grand Jeu.*

1929 Publication (in collaboration with Louis Aragon and
Man Ray) of *1929.*

1929– Residence in Brazil.
1931

1931 Joins the Liga Communista (Opposição). Birth of his son
Geyser. Imprisoned and expelled from Brazil for his
political activities.

1934 Publication of *De Derrière les fagots.*

1935 For the opening of an international Surrealist exhibition,
accompanies André Breton to Santa Cruz in the Canary
Islands, where he gives several lectures.

1936   Goes to Spain in August, to work with the P.O.U.M. and the P.O.I. Publication of *Je ne mange pas de ce pain-là, Je sublime,* and *Trois Cerises et une sardine.*

1937   March, serves on the Aragonese Front as an anarchist militiaman.

1938   Publication of *Au Paradis des fantômes.*

1940   Recalled to military service in February. Arrested for political activism in May. Imprisoned at Rennes. Released upon payment of a ransom to the German occupying forces. Lives in concealment in Paris until the end of the year. Succeeds in crossing into Unoccupied France, joining Breton and numerous friends in Marseilles.

1941   Leaves for Mexico.

1942   Publication of *Les Malheurs d'un dollar.*

1943   After the death of Elsie Houston, marries the painter Remedios. Publication of *La Parole est à Péret.*

1945   Publication of *Le Déshonneur des poètes* and *Dernier Malheur, dernière chance.*

1946   Under the pseudonym of Peralta, publishes *Manifeste des exégètes,* confirming his break with the IVth International. Publication of *Main forte.*

1947   Publication of *Feu central.*

1948   Returns to Paris, where he resumes work as a proofreader.

1949   Publication of *La Brebis galante.*

1952   Publication of *Air mexicain.*

1953   Publication of *Mort aux Vaches et au champ d'honneur* and (in collaboration with André Breton and Jindrich Heisler) of *Toyen.*

1954   Brief visit to Spain. Publication of *Les Rouilles encagées* (*Les Couilles enragées*), under the pseudonym Satyremont.

1955   Travels to Brazil, with stops at Rio de Janeiro and Saõ Paulo. Visits the Indians of the Amazon. Publication of his translation *Le Livre de Chilám Balám de Chumayel.*

1956   Publication of *Anthologie de l'Amour sublime.*

1957   Publication of *Le Gigot, sa vie et son œuvre.*

1958   Publication of *Histoire naturelle* and of the anthology *La poesia surrealista francese.*

1959   Dies in Paris.

Chronology

1960   Publication of *Anthologie des Mythes, légendes et contes populaires d'Amérique*.

1962   Publication, by some of his friends, of *De la part de Péret*; foundation of the Association des Amis de Benjamin Péret.

1963   Publication of *Dames et Généraux*.

1965   Publication (in collaboration with G. Munis) of *Pour un Second Manifeste Communiste*.

1968   Publication of *Les Mains dans les poches* and (in collaboration with G. Munis) of *Les Syndicats contre la Révolution*.

CHAPTER 1

A Man All of a Piece

I *Without Restraint into the Poetic Adventure*

EVEN before the death of André Breton in 1966, critics had begun to show signs of agreeing that it was time to grant Surrealism serious attention. More often than not, however, their efforts have given substance to misgivings underlying doleful predictions from within the Surrealist group that, one day, "the professors" would presume to interpret in their own fashion an undertaking never meant to appeal to their taste. So far as such critics may flatter themselves that they have made progress with Surrealism, they have succeeded in doing so only in a certain direction and on a certain level. A few exceptions stand out, of course. Yet all in all, the evidence before us speaks for itself. Restriction of the period of Surrealist activity to the twenties and thirties, at the expense of Surrealist effort during the following three decades, is no less revelatory of an instinct to misrepresent Surrealism than is the inclusion of Jean Cocteau —that "cheat," as Philippe Soupault has called him[1]—among exponents of Surrealism in the cinema.

Modification and even unequivocal distortion of Surrealism's aims, as well as of its accomplishments, confirm that, so far as handling the products of Surrealist endeavor is concerned, a selective principle has been operative in critical circles. This principle has had a variety of results, none of them fruitful. Not the least significant of these has been neglect of Benjamin Péret by virtually all who claim to address themselves to Surrealism's contribution in the field of creative writing. Nothing could be more striking, in this connection, than the contrast between the treatment generally accorded Péret by the critics and his reputation within Surrealism. To the Surrealists, Péret's work stands un-

17

rivaled. On the other hand, among critics the attitude of Eric
Sellin seems typical. In Sellin's eyes, an attempt to give Péret
something approaching his due is tantamount, apparently, to an
open admission of faulty judgment.[2] Exceptional indeed is Henri
Peyre's comment that Péret is "one of the greatest poets of the
age."[3]

This, in fact, is the crucial point that makes Péret so interesting. When André Breton praised him in 1952 for being, of
all the Surrealists, the one who had thrown himself without
restraint into the poetic adventure,[4] he firmly underlined the
value of Péret's work, in the context of Surrealism. The important thing for us to notice is that Péret's preeminence among
Surrealist writers is indicative of his success in coming closer
than anyone else to attaining the Surrealist ideal in poetry. His
rejection by literary commentators, meanwhile, betrays their
reluctance—and in some cases their inability—to respond to that
ideal and to weigh its consequences for poetic expression.

Allegiance to Surrealism engendered in Péret a special form
of responsibility. It required him to liberate himself from the
kind of obligation under which poetry traditionally had placed
its practitioners. At the same time, it imposed upon him the
necessity to remain always at the disposal of that inner voice
which, Surrealists believe, finds clearest expression during a state
called *absence* by Breton and *vacancy* by Péret. To this state,
if we are to believe the *Manifesto of Surrealism* published by
Breton in 1924, the practice of verbal automatism most readily
promises access. Acknowledging Péret's superiority as a Surrealist therefore means beginning with the realization that, more
productively than anyone else, he succeeded in availing himself
of the benefits of automatic writing, as defined in the 1924
manifesto.

During the period prior to 1924 when some of the future
Surrealists experimented with mediumistic trance, "the period
of sleeping fits," as it came to be known, three men in particular distinguished themselves by the ease with which they entered
the state of *vacancy* that permitted them to utter dazzling,
irrational images: René Crevel, Robert Desnos and Benjamin
Péret. Indeed, Péret's conversion to automatism, as a younger
Surrealist, José Pierre, has noted, was "immediate" and led at

once to results that Pierre has not hesitated to characterize as "inimitable."[5] Nowhere, though, do we find in his writings any explanation of automatism or any justification for its use. If we are looking for theoretical arguments, we find these in Breton, not in Péret.

André Breton's definition of Surrealism, in the *Manifeste du surréalisme*, rested squarely upon the automatic principle: "Pure psychic automatism by which we propose to express, either verbally, or in writing, or in any other manner, the true functioning of thought. The dictation of thought in the absence of all control exercised by reason, outside all aesthetic or moral preoccupations." Consistently working according to this principle, Benjamin Péret was to obtain results that tend to elude classification and defeat evaluation by the standards customarily invoked during assessment of poetic endeavor. This is why Péret presents serious difficulties to anyone who considers these standards to be the only ones applicable to the measurement of a poet's stature. By the same token, his achievement must appear especially praiseworthy to someone who approves the departure from conventional poetic practice made possible in Surrealism by recourse to automatism.

II Poet and Revolutionary

Who was this man who brought to the expression of Surrealist ideals in their purest form an aptitude that set him above all those to whom the *Manifesto of Surrealism* was a rallying call?

In response to a questionnaire that asked how he had got his start in life, Benjamin Péret wrote, "The 1914 war, which made everything easy!" Joining the army at his mother's urging, he made the discovery of poetry in the form of a volume of Mallarmé's verse, found on a railroad station bench, between trains. Like others, including Breton, Aragon, Eluard, and Soupault, he returned to civilian life, in 1919, with an abiding hate for the military. And he could see no sense in pursuing a poetic career along the lines of Symbolism, in imitation of Mallarmé perhaps. It is no surprise, then, to learn what Breton has to say in his *Nadja*, referring to the time when he was coeditor of an antiliterary magazine ironically entitled *Littérature*:

Still on the Place du Panthéon, one evening, late. A knock at the door. In comes a woman whose approximate age and features escape me today. In mourning, I think. She asks for a copy of the review *Littérature* which has not yet come out and that someone has made her promise to bring back to Nantes, next day. She insists, to my great regret, upon having it. But she seems to have come above all to "recommend" to me the person who has sent her and who is to be coming to Paris soon, to settle (I recall the expression: "Who'd like to get started in literature" which, since then, knowing to whom it applied, I have found so strange, so moving). But whom was I being charged this way, in more than fanciful terms, with welcoming, with advising? A few days later, Benjamin Péret was there.[6]

There followed a period during which, bv Breton's side, Péret, "my dearest and oldest companion in the fight," as Breton calls him in *Entretiens* (209), was active in the cause of universal iconoclasm known as Dada. Legend has it that, in the course of a Dada event held at the Salle Gaveau in Paris, Péret shouted from out front, "Long live France and French fries!" In the celebrated mock trial of Maurice Barrès, conducted under Dada aegis in May, 1921, Benjamin Péret, as the Unknown Soldier, in French military uniform, was a witness for the prosecution, goose-stepping and responding to questions only in German. But like others—Aragon, Breton, Soupault—Péret tired of the unproductive negativity of Dada. In the fifth number of *Littérature* (October, 1922), he first analyzed Dada's weaknesses as he saw them and then declared, "I take off the Dada spectacles and, ready to leave, I look to see where the wind is coming from, without worrying over knowing what it will be or where it will take me." Of the former participants in Dada who enlisted in Surrealism, none was firmer in his condemnation of Dada than Péret, who, specifically, was to deny the continuity of Dada and Surrealist thought, asserted by some literary historians.[7]

December, 1924, saw the appearance of the first number of *La Révolution surréaliste*. "At the beginning," comments Breton in *Entretiens*, "the emphasis in the magazine falls on pure surrealism—surrealism, let us say, in its natural state—and this is what led to editorship being entrusted to Pierre Naville and Benjamin Péret, who could be regarded at this time as the most totally animated by the new spirit and the most rebellious against all concessions" (106). Naville and Péret edited *La Révolution surréaliste* jointly, up to and including the third issue, April 15, 1925. Thereafter Breton assumed direction. Naville was soon to leave the Surrealist movement, but Péret remained, a life-long participant, to widen his reputation as the most aggressive Surrealist of his generation, or any other.

"Our associate Benjamin Péret insulting a priest." Surely more people have heard of the snapshot that appeared over this legend in the eighth number of *La Révolution surréaliste* (December, 1928) than are acquainted with the contributions made by Péret to this and every subsequent Surrealist review. In the history of Surrealism, Péret's name survives generally as that of the man Victor Crastre has called "the 'musketeer' of surrealism," remembered not for his writings but for "wielding insult like a sword."[8] Unquestionably, it is unjust to present Péret exclusively in this light. All the same, there is some justification for being attentive to the side of Péret's activities that has appeared most conspicuous. Reproducing the well-known photograph more than thirty years later, the Surrealist Jehan Mayoux pointed out that, in adopting a combative posture, Péret took on a role that completed Breton's: "Simplifying a lot, one can say that Breton constructed surrealism from within, while Péret defines it and makes it known by opposing it to what is different."[9] Quite rightly Mayoux credits Benjamin Péret with fulfilling the function he had made his own, through his writings as well as through his actions. He just as accurately identifies the form of reprisal—a kind of conspiracy of silence, where his writings were concerned—that Péret brought down on his own head.

Something needs to be added, though, to what Mayoux has said, if Péret's public display of anticlericalism is not to be stripped of its true meaning. It is this: Péret's contempt for religion did not stem from an impulse to make a gesture in the spirit of provocation. In reality, it had the same origins as his poetic vocation.

In November, 1942, Péret wrote in Mexico a text published in New York in May of the following year, at the expense of some of his Surrealist friends. Called *La Parole est à Péret,* this text was intended to introduce an anthology of myths, legends, and

stories of the Americas.[10] It carried a statement that, apparently
lacking originality, looked innocent enough. Magic, declared
Péret, is the "flesh and blood of poetry." What is interesting,
however, is to see how Péret built on this foundation: "In the
myths and legends of the earliest periods ferment the gods who
will confine poetry to the straitjacket of religious dogmas, for
if poetry grows in the rich soil of magic, the pestilential miasmas
of religion rising from the same soil gave it a pale and sickly
hue, and it would have to raise its head above the noxious layer
to find its vigor once again."

Péret went on to argue that, having become the exclusive
domain of sorcerers, mythical poetry was condemned to ossifi-
cation in religious dogma. His contention was that in primitive
tribes having least contact with Western civilization, myths are
characterized not only by the relative absence of moral precepts
but also by "extreme poetic exuberance." Meanwhile, where
moral restrictions can be seen to be on the increase, poetic content is reduced. Accordingly, it should be self-evident that the
"repugnant" moral values of contemporary society are in conflict with poetry. Of those conservative values Péret wrote in
La Parole est à Péret, "Only the assistance of an immense
mechanism of material and intellectual coercion (the clergy and
the schools supporting the police and the law-courts) has allowed
them to stand until our time." It follows that release from
material and moral constraints will bring man new liberty, liberty of mind as well as liberty on the material plane.

It was Péret's conviction that nothing should be permitted to
come between man and attainment of such liberty, or at least
desire for it. He was especially alert, therefore, to the danger
of compromise. Hence his hate for religion found its strength
here. To his mind, religious belief survives only because "it
continues more or less to satisfy at bargain-basement prices a
need for the marvelous that the masses retain in the most
secret recesses of their being." In the measure that La Parole
est à Péret shows "religious consolation" and "the excitied pursuit of the marvelous" to be in conflict, it indicates that resistance
to religion was not, in Péret's eyes, merely an act of moral and
social significance, but also a protest made in the name of
poetry which he identified with the marvelous.

In view of what *La Parole est à Péret* has taught us, one way in which Péret's activities complemented Breton's is especially noteworthy. Like Breton, Péret soon felt the need to extend Surrealism's revolution to the plane of political action. Both joined the French Communist Party in 1927. The *drame du surréalisme*, as Crastre has called Surrealism's temporary alignment with political activism, was to leave Breton disenchanted with politics. But, although as a Trotskyist[11] Péret quickly came to see adamant resistance to Stalinism as imperative, he remained dedicated to the cause of revolution, working all his life as faithfully in that cause as in the cause of Surrealism. Appropriately, in his *Entretiens* Breton summons up the picture of Benjamin Péret, during the early days of the Spanish Civil War, seated rifle in hand, stroking a cat stretched out on his lap (178).[12]

In their prefatory note to the original edition of *La Parole est à Péret*, Benjamin Péret's Surrealist friends spoke of his life as "singularly pure of concessions." Later, *De la part de Péret* characterizes him as "of all the surrealist poets one of the most pure and the most subversive" (18). This collective text does not go so far as to equate pure poetry with subversion. Péret himself did do this, though, when remarking in *La Parole est à Péret*, "Just as the masters consider religion necessary to the people, so they judge that authentic poetry, which is in danger of helping to emancipate the people, is harmful not only to the people but to society as a whole, for they suspect its subversive value." Meanwhile, G. Munis, who knew Péret as a militant revolutionary and coauthored with him *Pour un Second Manifeste Communiste*,[13] paid him this posthumous tribute in *Alarma*, in October, 1959: "He never knew whether he was a revolutionary because he was a poet or a poet because he was a revolutionary. Something would have been missing in him, had he known, for the indivisibility of the spirit is the only source, uncontaminated, of his infinite radiance."[14] This statement by Munis calls for comment.

Few, if any, of those who worked with Péret as political revolutionaries knew that he was a poet, as they surely would have done had the substance of his writings been politically subversive. Meanwhile, it was certainly not as a poet that Péret was first jailed and then expelled from Brazil—where he had joined the Liga Communista (Oposição)—in 1931. And it was not Benjamin Péret the Surrealist writer who, arrested in France in May, 1940, was imprisoned at Rennes, and then bought his release by paying a ransom to the Germans.

It so happens that the episode just mentioned does receive some discussion in *La Parole est à Péret*. Such an allusion to personal experience is most exceptional in the writings of Péret, whose practice differed radically from Breton's in this respect. Whereas Breton repeatedly probed the meaning of his own life in texts like *Nadja*, through which he illuminated the Surrealist viewpoint and sensibility, Péret remained consistently one of the most discreet of Surrealists. It is inconceivable that Benjamin Péret would ever have written his memoirs, as Surrealists of his generation (Maxime Alexandre, Jacques Baron, André Thirion) have done. It is not that he was a secretive man so much as that his private life did not inform his writings in the way Breton's informed his. More important still, Péret never confused revolution on the political level with an activity he considered profoundly revolutionary, namely, poetry. And yet, as Jean Schuster observed when prefacing a volume that brought together *Le Parole est à Péret* and *Le Déshonneur des poètes* (1945), both forms of revolutionary action seemed necessary to Péret, who considered their "objective conciliation" to be premature.[15] The literature of commitment, as popularized by Jean-Paul Sartre, was a contradiction in terms to Péret, whose *Le Déshonneur des poètes* was a pitiless attack upon an anthology of French poets of the Resistance, among them the former Surrealists Louis Aragon and Paul Eluard: "Not one of these 'poems' attains a higher lyrical level than pharmaceutical publicity...." This broadside aimed at a certain concept of poetry expressed a point of view complemented by Péret's revolutionary principles, which have prompted Franklin Rosemont to declare, "In the quest for the Golden Fleece of Revolution, he will be the loser who does not, sooner or later, encounter the illuminating, immortal, intractable, and irreducible genius of Benjamin Péret."[16]

If then Jean-Louis Bédouin, who knew Péret well (yet did not learn for several years that his friend had been married to the Brazilian singer Elsie Houston) was correct in asserting that the poet and the militant revolutionary were inseparable in Péret, while never overlapping, so to speak,[17] why did Benjamin Péret refer to having been imprisoned, in *La Parole est à Péret?* The answer is to be found in the text. We do not see Péret pause over the reasons for his arrest, although these are mentioned.[18] Instead, he directs our attention to an experience he had in prison that elicits in *La Parole est à Péret* the following declaration, which, as we have seen, will find an echo in *Le Déshonneur des poètes*: "No pharmacist's prescription permits us to manufacture the marvelous." In other words, it was not to talk about himself as a revolutionary subversive that Péret alluded to his stay in Rennes. His purpose was to direct attention to an experience he considered essential to his primary task in *La Parole est à Péret*, namely explaining something in which, as a Surrealist poet, he identified the key to poetic action: the marvelous.

The pattern is a highly consistent one, far more so than might be inferred from a reading of Breton's *Entretiens,* which tells us, "During the three years that precede the new war [in 1939], surrealism reaffirms its determination not to come to terms with the system of values advanced by bourgeois society. This determination is expressed with the maximum of intransigence and audacity in Benjamin Péret's collection *Je ne mange pas de ce pain-là*" (193). What Breton does not point out is that *Je ne mange pas de ce pain-là* is a unique work and that the year (1936) that saw publication of these poems, which lay a charge of dynamite against some of the pillars of society—the church and the army, notably—was also the year when, just six months later, Péret published his *Je sublime,* in which *Entretiens* salutes "love taken to incandescence" (141).

Because Péret was always true to his ideals, his existence followed an unchanging course on the material plane also, eloquent testimony to his fidelity to principles that admitted of no compromise. Before war began in 1939, he made an unsuccessful attempt to obtain a passport so that he could go to Mexico. Upon his escape into Unoccupied France, after his prison term in Rennes, he found himself denied entry into the United States because of his political record.[19] However, he managed

to get away from France on the last ship to Mexico. Leaving
for the United States via Martinique, Breton was to return to
Europe in 1946. Péret, though, was compelled to stay in the
New World by circumstances with which he was quite familiar.
He wrote Breton from Mexico City on March 27, 1947, "It's
true I've not written for a very long time but what's the use of
writing to give always discouraging news: abominable material
circumstances, no hope of prompt return." On October 13 of
the same year, he confided, "I still can't make any arrangements
to return, for lack of money. As soon as this is possible, I'll let
you know."²⁰ When finally his friends had raised funds to bring
him back to France, he was able to return at last to Paris, where
he resumed the kind of life to which he was accustomed.
Someone who first met him in his later years has described
him in these terms: "Dear Benjamin Péret, faithful and loyal
to Breton to his last breath—maybe the only one of the group.
His material struggle (didn't he work in a typography place?).
And he lived in a walk-down room, underground, and for a
reason I forget was always full of coal dust. No money. A man
who truly lived in the high places (hauts lieux)."²¹

Eking out a living as a proofreader, Péret was never a public
figure, in the way that some of those he had known in Surrealism
(Aragon, Char, Eluard) were destined to become. He realized
and accepted without regret that the kind of poet he must
be could never find general acceptance in twentieth-century
society. In La Parole est à Péret, he wrote, "We know that the
status of poet automatically places the person who lays valid
claim to it on the fringe of society and does so in the measure
that he is more truly a poet." Moving from the general to the
particular, we may note that, as Jean-Louis Bédouin has remarked sagely, "One loves Péret; or else one detests him. One
feels in agreement with him immediately, or there is every
chance one never will be" (74).

We shall have to return to ask why this should be so. For the
moment, let us simply notice that André Breton once confided,
when writing of Péret, "I speak of him from too close up, as
of a light that, day after day, for thirty years, has made my
life look brighter."²² And let us recall, too, the obituary that
appeared in Les Lettres françaises on September 24, 1959:

Remaining to the end of his days André Breton's companion, in the successive developments of surrealism, he embodied the extreme expression of that movement for more than thirty-five years. A certain violence, even more than obscurity, may turn many people away from him. But it is certain that the history of poetry during those years cannot be written unless we take that violence into account as a poetic element.

CHAPTER 2

Poetic Principles

I *The Modest Recording Instrument*

A NOTE that appeared in *L'Express* on October 1, 1959, affirmed just after Péret's death, "Of all the surrealists Péret was perhaps the most faithful to the subject matter of violence and revolt upon which the movement was based. Perhaps he was, to the end, the most *authentically surrealist*." *L'Express* could be accused of having done Péret's memory a disservice by perpetuating the myth that Benjamin Péret deserves to be remembered more as the *mauvais garçon* of Surrealism in France than as its finest poet. Its obituary voices no reservations, it is true, so that such an interpretation of its intent may seem to betray unwarranted susceptibility. All the same, with Péret unwitting distortion must be resisted as vigorously as that of the deliberate kind. For Péret's case is a special one.

Author of an essay that tries to show, by way of a study of Péret's poetry, "how surrealism effectively contributes to the liberation of man," Jean-Christophe Bailly[1] has noted pertinently that there is in Péret's verse collections a remarkable continuity, "such that it becomes a problem that calls for solution in relation to the tradition that requires poets to 'evolve'" (21). Just as important is Bailly's observation that none of the mannerisms of literary effort are present in Péret's writings: "everything the first manifesto threw out never existed for Péret." Hence, in Péret's work, the Surrealist theory of the poetic image and "the exaltation of inspiration," as Bailly calls it, become most evident and "institute with the greatest clarity surrealism's break with the past." Hence the treatment Péret has received from almost every one of the critics who have taken the trouble to read his work is consistent with the widespread tendency to limit Surrealism to a restricted and carefully controlled role

28

in the evolution of twentieth-century art and literature. It demonstrates that most literary commentators are incapable of appreciating what Surrealists understand by poetry.

When a fellow Surrealist, Jehan Mayoux, points out that, in the poetry of that "pure poet" Benjamin Péret, "the contribution of the artist, I mean of the fabricator, of the artisan, is negligible," implicit in his evaluation is a concept of poetry that sets Péret's work outside the limits within which literary criticism has the right to apply its standards. Primarily, therefore, the striking discrepancy between the Surrealists' reaction to Péret and the way his work is assessed from the standpoint of literature signals a fundamental difference in approach. The latter warns us that we cannot hope to weigh Péret's achievement until we understand his poetic ideals well enough to see why treating his writings as literature is, and must continue to be, an unproductive activity.

Péret's opposition to inherited poetic forms was imperious, uncompromising, and unrelenting. Yet it rested upon no concerted plan for replacing old forms with new ones. Everything, it seems, followed naturally from his dismissal of the reflective process in favor of the spontaneity that automatism guarantees. There is nothing unexpected in this. More worthy of notice, surely, is the fact that Péret was not able to identify his poems as his own when he heard them read aloud. Those of us who think of the work of Benjamin Péret as instantly recognizable, in content and structure too, may feel it paradoxical that this should have been so. But, for that very reason, Péret's reaction is particularly deserving of attention.

As Breton foresaw when first advocating its use, verbal automatism by no means precludes individuality in writing. All the same, the effect of natural impulse, in giving form to the language of Surrealism, is quite different from the implementation of a literary technique, deliberately applied. Failure to recognize his own work was symptomatic of a profoundly characteristic trait in Péret: his complete freedom from a proprietary attitude toward his writings. This trait is important to notice, since in one respect at least it made Benjamin Péret unique among the first-generation Surrealists.

Paul Eluard's creative urges tended to centralize poetic ex-

perience upon the satisfaction of demands making themselves
felt within himself. All that is typical of his Surrealist poetry
testifies, therefore, to a rearrangement of elements borrowed
from the world of familiar reality and brought together in a
new order, under the influence of the poet's private needs. Much
the same may be said of André Breton, who in his verse
habitually fell into the role of intermediary between the reader
and the world of the surreal. The first-person mode in well-
known poems like his "Vigilance" and "Ode à Charles Fourier" is
no more significant in this connection than the possessive
pronouns that recur throughout his "L'Union libre." Authority
rests everywhere with the poet, whose posture before the world
that his work depicts accounts for the way he makes us see
things. As for Robert Desnos, with the verbal experiments of
L'Aumonyme (1923) and *Langage cuit* (1923) behind him, he,
too, resorted to the first-person perspective in *A la Mystérieuse*
(1926) and *Les Ténèbres* (1927). Louis Aragon, of course, was
aggressively egocentric in all his Surrealist verse. In a sense,
then, all these early Surrealist poets turned to an approach that
was essentially traditional in character. They challenged their
readers to accept the viewpoint of the writer, to see the world
as his experience made him see it, and hence to share in the
emotional excitement and imaginative release engendered by
that experience. This is to say that the presence of the poet,
to which the distinctive tone of his voice makes us sensitive,
justifies all that he has to show us. We are brought face to face
with a creative sensibility animated by personal feelings that,
in the best tradition of lyrical poetry, inspired Eluard, for
example.

Péret has something different to offer. For the most part,
his work eludes the controls normally imposed upon the creative
process by the poet's need to satisfy the demands of an ego
ever ready to display itself for the admiration of others. A
special kind of modesty pervades his writings. Characteristically,
he declines to take up a central position in his poems. Instead,
he either celebrates the beauty of woman in texts where he is
content to bear witness to the miracle of love, or he evokes a
world which to some of his readers must appear impertinent or
frivolous, precisely because he betrays no inclination to relate

what he shows us to the familiar by way of a personal reaction. Typically, beneath the title "Mémoires de Benjamin Péret," he opens one of his poems with the words:

> Un ours mangeait des seins
> Le canapé mangé l'ours cracha des seins
> Des seins sortit une vache
> La vache pissa des chats
> Les chats firent une échelle

> A bear was eating breasts
> The sofa eaten up the bear spat out breasts
> From the breasts emerged a cow
> The cow pissed cats
> The cats made a ladder
>
> *(Le Grand Jeu,* 1928)

Whether we understand *canapé* as a sofa or as a slice of bread fried in butter (or even, preferably, as both at the same time— this is Péret's universe, not the world we are accustomed to see about us), we still face the fact that nothing in the opening of "Mémoires de Benjamin Péret" or in the rest of the poem seems to keep the promise of its title, according to the traditions of confessional poetry. One critic, indeed, can detect here nothing but "disorder," and goes on to refer vaguely to a lyricism that he can find only now and again in Péret's work, in *Dormir, dormir dans les pierres* (1927) and in *Je sublime* (1936).[2] On the other hand, Pierre Naville—obviously protesting against the conventional notion of lyricism—denies that there is any in the writings of Benjamin Péret.[3] Evidently, one can speak of Péret's lyricism, as it infuses all his work, only if one is prepared to revise one's definition of the lyrical element in poetry.

Because he did not feel possessive about the things he wrote, Péret was all the better able to assume the role of witness to poetic manifestation, as he understood the term, and so to become, beyond question, the most faithful of the "modest *recording instruments*" —as Breton's 1924 manifesto described the Surrealists. Quite indifferent to the mannerisms that, in his opinion, pass for style, Péret was always at liberty to start anew and to discover in his poems the prompting of verbal automatism in the very process of consigning them to paper.

It is clear that the nature of Péret's undertaking will go on being difficult to pinpoint until we know what he writes about and why. What, one may ask, is this thing we have heard him call the marvelous? How does it relate to a concept of poetry that appears singularly elusive? No hard-and-fast answers are readily available to permit us to send a mildly curious but impatient reader away with convenient one-sentence answers to these questions. Our difficulties are compounded by the fact that, as might be anticipated, Péret never took the trouble to indicate how the ideas on poetry he set down on paper related to his own work. The most he ever did was allude to the principle that he took to be fundamental to poetic activity, leaving his readers free to infer their own conclusions about his approach to poetic creation from what he told them. So reticent was he that the public may be forgiven for deeming Benjamin Péret content with generalizations which, on the surface anyway, scarcely promise to infuse his publications, whether they be creative or interpretive, with noteworthy originality. He began his celebrated attack on patriotic verse, *Le Déshonneur des poètes*, with the characteristic assertion that poetry is the very breath of man, and with the declaration that in poetry the spiritual life of humanity is condensed.

One consequence of the approach Péret adopted in his writings about poetry may be seen in Mary Ann Caws's study of Dada and Surrealist poets. Defending her choice of the writings of Aragon, Breton, Desnos, and Eluard for examination, Mrs. Caws remarks, "The other poets connected with the two movements do not appear to demonstrate the same strength in poetry and in critical thinking: for example, Péret's poetry is magnificent, as is generally agreed, but his theoretical work tends toward the simplistic."[4] There are times when it seems that Péret's sense of humor led him to invite just such a criticism. But the truth of the matter lies elsewhere.

II   *The Marvelous and Poetry*

On the subject of poetry, Benjamin Péret wrote as though he felt he had only to remind his audience of self-evident truths that needed neither discussion nor defense, too fundamental to meet serious objection. The tone is stern in *Le Déshonneur des poètes* but by no means as aggressive as might be expected of a man who showed no reluctance to admit to the following peculiarities: "detests priests, cops, Stalinists, and tradespeople." And so a distinctive feature of the texts in which Péret speaks of the essential characteristics of poetry is the mingling of apparently banal statements with others, given no more stress or development than the former, that are very difficult to follow sometimes and that lie at the source of Péret's motivation as a poet. What, for instance, does he mean when, on the first page of *Le Déshonneur des poètes,* he calls poetry "the source of all knowledge and that knowledge itself in its most immaculate aspect?" Students of Surrealism will have no trouble recognizing the orthodoxy of Péret's basic principles, seen from the standpoint of Surrealism, which from its inception equated poetic action with the act of cognition. But this still does not take us all the way to our ultimate goal: definition of the contribution that Péret's idea of poetry led him to make within the framework of Surrealism. We shall come much nearer to that goal if we begin by facing a question important enough to Péret to provoke him, against custom, into personal reminiscence in *La Parole est à Péret.* This is the question of the significance of the marvelous and, specifically, of what, in Péret's estimation, it represents in poetry.

La Parole est à Péret provides a convenient and reliable starting point for an examination of what may be termed, very approximately, Péret's theory of the marvelous. This text shows how far he is willing to go on the theoretical plane and lets us know unequivocally at which point he is prepared to stop. "It is expected no doubt that I will define the poetic marvelous. I shall take good care not to do so. It is of a luminous nature that does not suffer competition from the sun: it disperses shadows and the sun dulls its brilliance. The dictionary, of course, confines itself to giving its dry etymology in which the marvelous can be recognized with as much difficulty as an orchid preserved in a herbarium. I shall try only to give a suggestion of it" (33–34).

To Benjamin Péret, obviously, the important thing is not defining the marvelous so much as experiencing it, acknowledging its ever-presence and its disruptive effect: "However, the marvelous is everywhere, hidden from the eyes of the vulgar, but ready to explode like a time bomb." Returning to emphasize this point, he equates the marvelous with life itself—"on condition though that it does not render life deliberately sordid as society strains its ingenuity to do with its schools, religion, law-courts, wars, occupations and liberations, concentration camps, and horrible material and intellectual wretchedness." It is only now that, having linked the marvelous to the spirit of anticonformity, Péret alludes to his period of confinement at Rennes.

He reports that one day he discovered the window of his cell had been painted over. In each of its four panes, he could now make out an evocative shape. From day to day these pictures would appear to change, only one of them seeming invariably the same: the figure 22, which had convinced him he would be freed on the 22nd of a month as yet unknown. After his release—it occurred on July 22, 1940—Benjamin Péret tried his hand at painting window panes, but without producing interesting results. The marvelous cannot be manufactured, he now realized: "It grabs you by the throat. A certain state of 'vacancy' is needed for the marvelous to deign visit you."

This statement is of the greatest importance, sparing us the temptation to set off in the wrong direction, in our search for the meaning of the marvelous in his work. Within Surrealism, Benjamin Péret does not rank as the most admirable of poets just because he was the one who most closely and most consistently respected the recommendations concerning automatic practices set forth in the *Manifeste du surréalisme*. Such a claim to fame would rest upon the notion of poetry as mere technique, as a recipe available to all but applied best by the writer best equipped to follow it most faithfully. In this connection, we cannot overstress Louis Aragon's remark that, if one writes idiotic things according to the Surrealist method, they are no less idiotic for that. The automatic method was promoted within the Surrealist movement as a means of releasing inspirational resources, not as an excuse for forgiving those in whom these resources proved to be inadequate. Thus Péret did not gain preeminence among the Surrealist poets merely by his willingness to rely on automatism, but because automatic writing enabled him to offer a perspective upon reality that was uniquely his. It would be futile to try analyzing his work in the hope of learning how to write like Péret. As Péret understood and practiced it, poetry lies in a viewpoint upon the world, not in a method for dealing with it. And it is in probing the idea of the marvelous that we have most chance of explaining what that viewpoint was and how it is communicated through his writings.

Allusions to the marvelous remain discreet in *La Parole est à Péret*. And there are none at all to be found in the pages, written in São Paulo in August, 1955, added to the 1942 text so that it could preface Péret's *Anthologie des Mythes, légendes et contes populaires d'Amérique*. This is because in his mind poetry and the marvelous are one. Speaking of the former necessarily means referring to the latter, especially when poetry is being discussed in its revolutionary function:

It fell to romanticism to find the marvelous once again and to endow poetry with a revolutionary significance that it still retains today and that allows it to live an outlaw existence, but to live all the same. For the poet—I'm not speaking of amusers of every sort—cannot be acknowledged as such if he does not oppose the world in which he lives with total nonconformism. (*La Parole est à Péret*, 65).

Coming after a succession of statements that insist upon the inevitably revolutionary role of poetry, these words establish the basis for our appreciation of Péret's writings: that the marvelous is a sign of social and moral anticonformity, signaling unyielding resistance to accepted social modes of thought and feeling. It measures the poet's difference, his distance from a society by which he does not seek acceptance. This is the sense in which we are to take the declaration in *La Parole est à Péret* to the effect that the poet of today has "no other resource than to be a revolutionary or not to be a poet." Fulfilling this role meant, to Péret, "ceaselessly plunging into the unknown." This is to say that "there are no gilt-edged investments, but risk and adventure renewed indefinitely." Only in this way, Péret was convinced, can the poet call himself a poet and "claim to take a legitimate place in the very forefront of the cultural movement, where he can earn neither praise nor laurels but strike with all his might to level the barriers raised time after time by stupidity and routine." Indeed the poet's situation as an outsider is proof of his authenticity: "The curse thrown at him by present-day society already indicates his revolutionary position; but he will shed his obligatory reserve in order to see himself placed at the head of society when, completely turned upside down, it has recognized the common origin of poetry and knowledge and when the poet, with the active and passive cooperation of everyone, creates the exciting marvelous myths that will send the whole world to the assault of the unknown."

These words, with which *La Parole est à Péret* comes to a close, may appear more enthusiastic than persuasive. To be given their full weight, they need to be considered in the light of a basic assumption upon which the whole essay rests: that mankind has "a thirst for the irrational" which, as we would expect, Péret bitterly regretted seeing channeled by religious faith. It seemed logical to Benjamin Péret that eliminating religion would result in releasing the need for the irrational, "*les élans irrationnels*" being latent in all men. It appeared to him no less logical that, in men deprived of the irrational, this need would find satisfaction through the marvelous, and not through the—to him—false substitute of religious faith.

Now it is possible to comprehend why all the information we have gathered so far concerning the poetic marvelous found its way into an essay intended to present an anthology of myths, popular legends, and folktales. It was Péret's belief that in earlier days man could think "only in the poetic mode," and that, in consequence, he could "penetrate perhaps intuitively farther" into himself and into nature, "from which he was scarcely differentiated," than the rationalist thinker who starts out from book learning in his attempt to dissect nature. A point upon which *La Parole est à Péret* insists, therefore, is that rationalist thought is mistaken, in holding poetry in contempt:

And so long as we have not recognized without reticence the capital role of the unconscious in psychic life, its effects on the conscious and the latter's reactions to the former, we shall continue to think as priests, that is to say as dualist savages, with this reservation, however, that the savage remains a poet while the rationalist who refuses to understand the *unity* of thought remains an obstacle to cul-

tural movement. He who does understand it shows himself to be a
revolutionary who tends, perhaps unwittingly, to rejoin poetry.
(31–32)

Prolonging this attack upon the "artificial opposition," created
by sectarian minds "from both sides of the barricade," between
poetic thought and logical thought, between rational and irrational thought, *La Parole est à Péret* asks:

If the man of yesterday, knowing no other limits in his thinking than
those of his desires, was able, in his struggle with nature, to produce
these marvelous legends, what cannot be created by the man of
tomorrow, conscious of his nature and dominating the world more
and more with a mind freed of all impediments? (61)

Obviously, the question is rhetorical. In asking it, Péret foresaw no reluctance on his readers' part to agree with the *movement* of his own thought. However, his thinking still lacks
sufficient clarity to dispose of all reservations, even in those whose
natural inclination may be to accept the line of reasoning underlying *La Parole est à Péret*. We still need to examine another
text of his. This is an article that appeared in February, 1944, in
the fourth number of the American Surrealist magazine *VVV*,
under the title "La Pensée est UNE et indivisible."[5]

III *"Thought Is ONE and Indivisible"*

Falling chronologically between *La Parole est à Péret* and
Le Déshonneur des poètes, Benjamin Péret's 1944 article estab-
lishes the continuity of his thought beyond a shadow of a doubt.
It opens with a reference to the eighteenth century as, in France,
the century of rationalist thought and hence as a period that
saw only one poet worthy of mention—the Marquis de Sade,
who revolted against the essential postulates of the era in which
he lived. As Péret's text speaks of it, Sade's revolutionary role—
and hence, of course, his claim to the rank of poet—was to challenge the eighteenth century's effort to replace one mode of blind
faith, religion, with another, no less fallacious in Péret's estimation: reason.

True, the so-called Age of Enlightenment had eliminated God,

"the obstacle to all knowledge." But, having substituted another
deity, it had to be opposed. And opposition could come, in Péret's
view, only from a poet. Sade merits the title of poet, therefore,
not as a writer of verse—Péret's ideas in broadening the application of the term well beyond limitations of a literary nature
were entirely consonant with Surrealist teaching—but because
he met criteria specified in *Le Déshonneur des poètes*: "An
inventor for whom discovery is but the means for attaining a
new discovery, without respite he must fight the paralyzing gods
bent on keeping man in servitude to social powers and divinity
that complement one another. He will therefore be a
revolutionary. . . ."

Behind Péret's confidence in the poet as a revolutionary lies
trust in political convictions of no particular kind, faith in no
plan for social reorganization of utopian character. Rather, his
reliance on the poet as the agent of revolution reflects unshak-
able trust, expressed in *VVV*, in poetry as "the source and crown
of all thought." Under reason's tutelage, however, poetry is subject to distortion. This is because, evidently, the marvelous,
"heart and nervous system of all poetry," has been rejected.
Where reason has not been "cast down from its celestial throne,"
the marvelous will always be treated in this fashion, Péret believed. And so this is why the peculiar accent of the individual
poet's voice—even of his own voice—impressed Benjamin Péret
not at all. He was attentive, instead, to intimations of a collective
impulse to challenge the world of reason through the release
of imaginative forces that he took to be universal in effect. Hence
his abiding interest in myths, folklore, and legend, all of which
pay homage to the salutary power of imagination, without taking into account the contribution made by individuals in testifying to that power. In Péret the imaginative liberation of natural
phenomena, as the substance of poetry, occurred all the more
readily, it would seem, because the writer was subject to no
inclination to disrupt the familiar universe in order to satisfy
selfish desires. It was Eluard who, as a Surrealist, was most
frequently given to citing Lautréamont's dictum, "Poetry will
be made by all, not one." But it was Péret who most consistently
worked in the light of the principle that Eluard invoked.

Alluding to a poem by Paul Eluard, "Liberté," said to have

been dropped over occupied France during leaflet raids by the Royal Air Force, Péret does not deign to mention it by name, when closing *Le Déshonneur des poètes*. His comments render exact identification superfluous: "Any 'poem' that exalts a 'liberty' deliberately undefined, when it is not decorated with religious or nationalist attributes, first ceases to be a poem and then constitutes an obstacle to the total liberation of man, for it deceives him by showing him a 'liberty' that conceals new chains. On the other hand, from every *authentic* poem emanates a breath of liberty, total and efficacious, even if that liberty is not evoked in its political and social aspect, and, in this way, contributes to the effective liberation of man."

In a world dominated by reason, the position of the poet is necessarily that of an adversary. More precisely, for its disruptive nature, that which Péret termed in 1944 "poetic intuition" continues to be regarded with enmity. Hence, to Péret's mind, the discredit under which prophetic intuition has fallen among the "blind followers of rationalist thought." Thus poetry as described in *Le Déshonneur des poètes*—"understood as total liberation for the human mind"—is a commodity for which there is no demand, and the poet has no place in society as long as he "fights to attain a forever perfectible knowledge of himself and the universe."

Of necessity, the poet must resist accepting the scale of values established by conscious reality, as described in Péret's essay in *VVV*: "the rational product of absurd and horrible social constraints." This means that the poet must recognize consciousness as "always in the wrong from the point of view of the necessities of man and of his development," while the unconscious is to be acknowledged as "the seat of desire, the sovereign phoenix engendered indefinitely from its own ashes."[6] To be able to do this, the poet has to realize that the unacceptable values are the ones perceived "through the deforming prism of rationalist education," which treats intuition as a caretaker, when in reality, according to Péret, it is "the engineer who directs operations, the only man of science, the great inventor, the creator of reason itself."

At the source of Péret's argument lies the hypothesis that reason has usurped the power rightly belonging to intuition and now uses that power to crush intuition. Reestablishing the supremacy of intuition means, therefore, recognizing that intuition gave rise both to reason and to unreason. Abolition of all gods, including reason, entails understanding that "there is no thought without intuition, that is to say, without second sight, no intuition without thought." Thus the hypothesis upon which "La Pensée est UNE et indivisible" rests calls for reducing the role of reasoned thought and increasing that of poetic intuition. Such is the generally accepted trust in reason, however, that presuming to question its universal validity may appear an open invitation to madness and disorder. Thus, attaining the balance demanded by Benjamin Péret in 1944 can pass for evidence of imbalance, or at least an unacceptable predisposition toward it. As Louis Aragon once put it:

The marvelous opposes what exists mechanically, what *is* so much it isn't noticed any more, and so it is commonly believed the marvelous is the negation of reality. This rather summary idea is conditionally acceptable. It is certain the marvelous is born of the refusal of *one* reality, but also of the development of a new relationship, of a new reality that this refusal has liberated.[7]

Responsiveness to the marvelous, as Péret's theoretical writings speak of it, is quite impossible until we appreciate that the refusal emphasized by Aragon stands for something very different from escapist fancy. Intuition opposed to rationalist thought, finding encouragement in a spirit of liberty that takes no account of the social, moral, and political customs of contemporary society is the prime element in the marvelous as we shall see it celebrated in Péret's poetic writings. Here the marvelous confronts us with a variety of inherited and inculcated prejudices and predispositions, all of them unacceptable from the standpoint of poetry, as Péret understood it. Does then the marvelous lose, in the process, its ability to elicit the wonder, pleasure, excitement, joy, and dread that were so much a part of the folk literature Péret admired? Hardly. This is a question that can be asked with some degree of seriousness only by someone who knows nothing about the direction Péret's theories led him to take and who is unacquainted with the universe of the marvelous to which his imagination supplied the key. It is a universe we may enter by way of his *Histoire naturelle*,[8] and explore not only through his verse but also through a novel, *Mort aux Vaches et au champ d'honneur* (Death to Cops and to the Field of Honor),[9] a succession of short stories, brought together under the improbable title *Le Gigot, sa vie et son œuvre* (The Leg of Mutton, its Life and Works),[10] and a separately published tale called *La Brebis galante* (The Gallant Sheep).[11]

CHAPTER 3

Myth: Histoire naturelle

I *Man Invents*

BENJAMIN Péret's work was never destined to reach a wide public during his lifetime. Following a trend characteristic of Surrealist publications, each of his verse collections appeared in a small printing. Even *Le Grand Jeu* came out with Gallimard in an edition of only 174 copies. However, with Gallimard as its publisher, that book did at least benefit from the services of a major Parisian house. No less than six of Péret's other volumes originally bore the imprint Editions surréalistes, in other words, they appeared as *La Parole est à Péret* did at the Surrealists' own expense. All the same, however small the printing, Péret's writings were always addressed to the public at large. Only one book stands as an exception to this rule. It is *Histoire naturelle,* of which Jehan Mayoux had 273 copies made in a noncommercial edition (253 copies of which were offered for sale by subscription only) boxed with Mayoux's *A Perte de vue.*

The circumstances of its publication in 1958 set *Histoire naturelle* apart from the rest of Péret's writings. Its contents, though, help guide us into the poetic universe that Benjamin Péret made his own, providing a practical illustration of the consequences of some of the ideas found in *La Parole est à Péret,* "Thought is ONE and indivisible," and *Le Déshonneur des poètes.* It is not difficult to see why this is so. The first texts of *Histoire naturelle,* "Les quatre éléments," are dated Mexico City, 1945—no more than three years after Benjamin Péret composed *La Parole est à Péret* as an introduction to his *Anthologie des Mythes* and less than a year, at most, after *Le Déshonneur des poètes.* These texts on the four elements were written, then, after Péret had been immersed in material from which he was to draw a four-hundred-page selection of myths, legends, and popular tales, under the impetus of a conception of the marvelous that, for him, distinguished honorable poets from dishonorable ones. "Le règne minérale," the second section of *Histoire naturelle*, was written in Paimpont in 1950 and both "Le règne végétal" and "Le règne animal"—the latter taking up about half of this sixty-page volume—were written in Paris in 1958. Nevertheless, *Histoire naturelle* remains from one end to the other true to the ideas we have heard Péret express.

After undertaking merely to suggest the marvelous, rather than define it, Péret wrote in *La Parole est à Péret*,

"I think of the dolls of the Hopi Indians of New Mexico, whose heads often schematically represent a medieval castle. It is into this castle that I wish to go. . . . Although I am apparently alone, a crowd blindly obedient to me surrounds me. These are creatures less distinct than a speck of dust in a ray of sunshine. In their heads of root, their will o' the wisp eyes move about in all directions and their twelve wings equipped with claws allow them to act with the rapidity of the lightning they bring in their wake. Out of my hand, they eat the eyes from peacock feathers and if I press them between thumb and forefinger, I mold a cigarette that, between the feet of a suit of armor, quickly takes the shape of the first artichoke" (34–35).

These lines lend weight to an early statement in the same context: "The bird flies, the fish swims and man invents, for alone in nature he is endowed with an imagination always on the alert, always stimulated by an ever-renewed necessity." *Histoire naturelle* expands upon the long passage we have just read and upon the explanation for it provided in *La Parole est à Péret*. It shows that invention was a poetic function for Benjamin Péret, and that poetic natural history may be governed by imaginative laws of myth-making that ignore scientific law.

Declaring that we may be sure that the explanations given by primitive man for the world and for his own origins are the product of pure imagination, with conscious reflection playing little or no part in the process, Péret takes care to cite A. H. Krapp, quoting T. Mommsen in his *La Genèse des mythes*: "Imagination is the mother of all poetry and of all history." Then he proceeds in *La Parole est à Péret* to attribute to these

circumstances the fact that primitive legend almost always has
its source in what he terms "the poetic marvelous." Primitive
man, he assures us, did not know himself and was searching for
himself. Modern man, in contrast, has lost his way. Is not the
implication that he will find it again, as primitive man searched
for himself, by prospecting the marvelous?

II   Antiscientific Natural History

Everything Péret had to say about primitive man, in contrast
with contemporary man, placed the advantage on the side of
the former. Not once do his writings give the impression that
primitive societies were, in his eyes, the object of mere curiosity,
and even less of strictly scientific interest. The introduction to
his *Anthologie des Mythes, légendes et contes populaires d'Amérique* gives early emphasis to the fact that his intention, when
preparing his selection, was not to encroach upon the domain
of ethnography, and for a very definite reason: "the poetic
criterion alone has presided over the choice of the texts making
up this book, and this mode of selection can only be arbitrary
from the point of view of any science."[1] At first this confession
may seem a token of becoming modesty on the part of a non-
specialist. In fact, it stands for something else. Benjamin Péret
looked upon myths as prefiguring both science and philosophy
and hence as "at the same time the first stage of poetry and the
axis about which it continues to turn at an indefinitely increasing speed." If, on the other hand, he was prepared to accept
science as born of a magic interpretation of the universe, Péret
was still persuaded that it "very closely resembles in any case
those children of the primitive horde who, according to Freud,
murdered their father."

After hearing Péret proclaim his disbelief in scientific explanations we have no cause to be surprised that *Histoire naturelle*
repudiates scientific interpretations of the origins of life and
the organization of the cosmos. And yet his texts ask the same
questions as science: How do things come into existence, by
what are they engendered? The focus of *Histoire naturelle* coin-
cides with that of natural history. Its answers to the same fundamental questions evidence radical differences, however. More
in agreement with the primitive's poetic intuition than with his

contemporaries' scientific mode of inquiry, Péret responds imaginatively. His *Histoire naturelle* is thus a retelling of the myth of creation, in a manner no less antiscientific than predictably antireligious.

Approaching this book from a scientific perspective, one is bound to find it chaotic. From the poetic standpoint adopted by Benjamin Péret, though, a sense of order subsists. Scientific relations and hypotheses are meaningless in a universe where the element fire adopts a variety of forms, one of the most common being stinking fire, "obtained by steeping a bishop in cod liver oil." Giving off a pestilential smell, fire in this form nevertheless is valuable, because it promotes the cultivation of asparagus: "for stinking fire destroys the drawers that gnaw at it as soon as it is born" (25).

Péret's humor is reflected not only in details of this kind but also in parody of scientific procedure throughout *Histoire naturelle*: a certain element, combined with another, or submitted to this or that process, gives . . . But parody is not an end in itself. Its effect is to show that poetic apprehension is limited neither by scientific demonstration nor by scientifically feasible hypothesis; that, to put it another way, the realm of poetry is not bounded by observable reality, submitted to rational interpretation. From this point of view, the special advantage of parodying natural history is the following. It submits to examination modifications in natural phenomena that result from changing conditions. As Péret finds change especially fascinating, he specifies conditions that, in the field of scientific inquiry, would lend validity to controlled experimentation. But, of course, the specifications his texts lay down do not conform at all to the ones meticulously imposed by science. The results are typified in his report upon the consequences of varying the conditions to which air may be subjected, in the world of the imagination. "Painted blue, air gives underbrush during dry weather and, in rainy weather, bleach, but then it is harmful to the man who absorbs it in large doses, for it provokes stomach ulcers and boils, and attacks tooth enamel" (16). How dry does the weather have to be? How wet? These questions—of paramount importance to the scientist and the audience to whom he addresses himself—are of less concern to the poet and those for whom he

writes than the results, since the latter are not scientifically pre-
dictable or verifiable, but imaginatively stimulating.

It is a noteworthy characteristic of the writing in *Histoire
naturelle* that the *movement* of Péret's sentences is distinctively
antiscientific. This is to say that the farther the sentence invites
us to follow, the greater the distance separating us in the
poetic domain from scientifically verifiable truth: "When the temperature drops below zero, well water is transformed into a
beggar who, cut into very thin slices, is used to make grottoes"
(21). This phenomenon is by no means confined to "Les quatre
éléments." We find it also in Péret's text about the mineral
kingdom, for instance. Here air, water, earth, and fire are
said to be amusing themselves: "They began then to mix, as the
fancy took them, all the minerals they had scorned up to then,
without forgetting to add every time a few drops of mercury,
and then were heard nothing but laughter and cries of joy that
sometimes would fly off, never to appear again, but often would
stay wheeling in great circles above them" (33).

Histoire naturelle displays no respect for the classifications
laid down by science. Hence the fact that it treats fire as an
essentially mineral element, resident in stones and eggs, has
scientifically unforeseeable consequences, when stones are found
to be subject to trembling. Their intermittent trembling causes
fire to cough and spit damp moss that extinguishes it, so giving
birth to fleas. These are fleas feared by dyers, on account of
their effect upon colors—which lose their brightness in the presence of fleas, becoming indistinguishable. The situation is not
without its compensations, though: mixing fleas and colors in
equal parts, in a sealed container, the mixture being kept at "a
fairly high temperature, for a variable time," gives either mot-
tling or moiré (23).

Since objective observation ceases to be pertinent in *Histoire
naturelle,* descriptive detail eludes the restrictions of observable
reality. Shut up in a closet, we are told, air tends to escape.
When it succeeds in doing so, it dies at the door, "in the form
of a mushroom in general use today against wrinkles" (16).
Evaporating sea water gives silk of astonishing longevity. It is
said there are female silks a thousand years old that still have
four litters of liqueur glasses a year, with a dozen glasses to

a litter. It is easy to see, Péret tells us, that, in these circumstances, liqueur glasses would have become a worse plague to man than locusts, if they had not found relentless enemies in crutches. Fortunately, each crutch annually devours dozens of thousands of liqueur glasses. The trouble is, though, that in equatorial Africa alone crutches—of which about twenty species have been identified—have eaten up all the liqueur glasses and are now the terror of the natives: destroying their veal-liver crops, crutches have reduced them to extreme poverty and famine.

III *The Principle of Causality, "Father of the Artichoke"*

Itemizing various forms of petroleum, Péret informs us that, under the action of sunshine, petroleum of the snows is transformed into a chair, and this chair is a lemur, inoffensive in appearance, yet with a venomous bite that can be fatal if the victim is not treated promptly (20). Under heat, well water hardens, we learn, expands, and at a precise temperature acquires great elasticity that renders it—who would have guessed?—apt to become a kangaroo in a few days (21). This process of transformation takes us every time in the same direction of unpredictability, finding its climax in the rationally inadmissible. And it follows the same development so often as to leave us in no doubt that the principle of causality had to undergo profound changes before it could be applied as it is in *Histoire naturelle*, where, soluble in oil, it is "the father of the artichoke" (20).

The accepted principle of derivation—of cause and effect—is set aside, ousted by the principle of marvelous derivation. When salted, air becomes a bed. Warmed between the hands, it expands until "metamorphosed into a whip" (16). Thus, as Péret speaks of them, derivations are mythical, poetic explanations that do not require authority in facts scientifically defined. And there is a wild logic here, showing that the way to obtain familiar products from unlikely ingredients is by scientifically inconceivable procedures. When watered, the earth gives a number of improbable phenomena. One of these is a Turkish bath which, obtained by kneading wet earth with curdled milk, makes so much noise it has to be packed off to a desert place

48 BENJAMIN PÉRET

(12). Spectacles for short-sighted people are to be obtained by softening earth in boiling China tea, before cooking in a double saucepan (12). Under other circumstances, earth gives lipstick, the compass, saveloy, the boxer, the match, the preposition, the frog that slowly devours the earth, and a cello frequently used for the treatment of arthritis.

In "Le règne minéral" we are informed that thunder striking limestone causes it to open "obsequiously" to let laurel burst forth (46). The same principle applies everywhere, even when Péret starts or ends up with an animal, instead of one of the elements or a natural phenomenon. In "Le règne animal" the dolphin is said to result from copulation between an attic and a Norwegian cooking pot (57). By combining and mixing diverse ingredients—trapeze, litote, sneezing powder, homeland, sergeant-major feather, etc.—the agave succeeds in extracting other dogs from a dog's tail. In white sauce, a giraffe gives a cormorant, when hot, and an ibis once it has cooled down. To extract crayfish and bears from it, one has to cut it into thin strips. Soaked in dirty oil, a giraffe gives a sparrow or a frigate, according to whether the sun is shining or whether it is a cloudy day (54).

Such derivations are not exclusively accessory details. They are incorporated into the narrative structure of "Le règne animal," which may be read as a direct response to the appeal issued in the *Manifeste du surréalisme* for "stories still almost fairy tales." Here we find: "And seizing a rule of three [the agave] plunged it into vinegar which began to sizzle, swearing, then to laugh in a silly way, assuming an inky shade. The monkey appeared and rushed to take a bath in the neighboring river, uttering sharp cries" (55–56). Later the agave makes the following statement: "From a liquified Archimedes' principle spiked with tomato sauce jelly, I built a turtle, but what disappointments it brought me! First it got mixed up with chenille, for the Archimedes' principle had evaporated when I took it out of the hollow of my hand. I had to rub it briskly with a metal brush until I'd given it a bluish glint, then feed it on proverbs for several months and finally dip it in copper filings to get it a shell that was presentable but so heavy the animal can no longer run, much less fly as I wanted" (58).

Repeatedly in "Le règne animal" Péret's imagination presents a challenge to the stability of the natural universe. More and more satisfied, the agave seizes a handful of salt that it throws into the calyx of a gladiolus, from which immediately bounds, "quite astonished," a codfish. Crushing a borage foot in a frenzy, it obtains a mole which plunges into the soil in search of cheese and gingerbread. Taking hold of a violin, the agave tunes it, and the instrument gives off waves of earthworms. When the agave plays a tune, a pig jumps from the bow, followed by a horse that runs off, frightened by the pig's grunting. "Enough music!" cries the rhododendron, snorting, thereby giving life to some kangaroos (53).

Personification is not a literary device in *Histoire naturelle*. Its use suggests much more strongly that inspiration has come from primitive mythology. To the Jivaro Indians, we remember, the sun is a man—as it is for the Chugach Eskimo—and the moon a woman, their relationships being those of humans. The Bororo Indians of the Brazilian Matto Grosso extend the animist conception to the whole universe. Benjamin Péret's comment in the introduction to his *Anthologie des Mythes* is especially enlightening, particularly for its reference to Breton's 1924 Surrealist manifesto: "But the richness and variety of cosmic interpretations invented by primitive men bear witness to the vigor and freshness of imagination in these peoples. They show they do not doubt that 'language has been given man so that he may make surrealist use of it.' "[2]

When Péret offers his version of the Creation in "Le règne minéral" the animating imagery he employs is not present so as to enliven a literary text. In fact, personification serves a non-literary purpose, as a subversive force that opposes scientific explanations with imaginative ones. Benjamin Péret does not practice anthropomorphism in *Histoire naturelle* as an adornment of literary value. Had he wished to do so, then surely he would have taken care to confine its use within acceptable literary bounds, instead of giving imagination free reign to draw his narrative into areas which common sense must judge to be those of the ridiculous and the ludicrous. Thus when the earth blows on a few globules of mercury, the result is so unhoped for that it takes the earth's breath away, leaving it with its mouth hanging open (32). Literary tradition accepts readily enough the technique of animating nature by allusions to its breathing. However, Péret's imagination is submitted to no censorship by literary convention when it logically proceeds to conceive of nature as a breathing organism left with its mouth open.

In some situations, as we have seen, the result of personification may be enrichment of the disruptive humorous effect created by *Histoire naturelle*. Elsewhere, its contribution is to bring Péret's text much closer to certain folktales that convey dread before menacing forces that man cannot control: "The wind, in one gust, carried off the potato, the turnip, and the onion, which were methodically getting drunk at the top of an oak tree, and buried them, while the same gust caught up, in a wild round dance, the plum tree, the maple, and the chestnut tree that were jostling everything in their path, provoking a bloody scuffle during which the carrot, skinned alive, was thrown into a hole and the plane tree was so soundly thrashed that it remained covered with ecchymosis" (46). A prickly pear is suddenly entangled in a jasmin whose howls of pain terrify a Virginia creeper, climbing a rock. As a result, the Virginia creeper loses all its leaves (45). Various stones, including granite, porphyry, and lava, tremble with terror: "They had good reason to." Rain, falling heavily, promotes germination. Thus is born, in tears, the marshmallow, which judges the inconsolable reseda: "Behave yourself, please!" At the same time the elm, still young, is gamboling about, looking for somewhere to put down its roots, pursued by ivy, full of hate: "You'll not get away from me. I'll have your hide" (43).

IV   *Singular Coupling*

Whether animism provokes amusement or not, one noteworthy feature of its use is that it finds support in descriptive detail, giving the ring of truth to imagination's inventions. In "Le règne minéral," for example, occurs a short passage that incorporates two comparisons borrowed from the familiar world to assist us in visualizing the world of imaginative creation: "The earth was the first to see rise from its hands, pot-bellied as a prosperous shopkeeper, well-groomed, freshly shaved and in Sunday best, big-eyed mica that, exclusively preoccupied with correcting its posture, fell victim to such bad luck that it collapsed like an overripe cheese" (34).

The interesting thing about this sentence and similar ones is that none of them reflects a serious attempt to reconcile the real and the imaginary. On the contrary, reality is introduced only in a way that highlights what is imagined, so making the latter self-sufficient. Witness the "terrible panther of knife blades, called flabbergasted panther," in "Le règne animal." It hangs around railroad stations at night, eating up switches (57). We gain a completely wrong estimate of the value Péret attached to the marvelous, if we do not realize that, far from wishing to submit his writing to the reality principle, he was well content to see reality's center of gravity shift, under the pull of imagination. Hence, familiar aspects of the known world receive at best ironic acknowledgment in *Histoire naturelle*: "A few moments later," we read in "Le règne minéral," "from this spot was born the artichoke which soon rose to a height of thirty feet then, noting its error, prudently went down again until it attained its normal size" (42).

The concessions Péret seems prepared or constrained to make before the demands of the familiar world are not concessions at all. His imagination takes reality into account just long enough to betray scorn for its claims. Thus the confession that unicorn petroleum is of no use as petroleum is but a prelude to this declaration: "Only its horn, decomposing under the action of the wind, gives birth to the sprinter, constantly used in the porcelain industry for purifying kaolin, which they first clean before anything else by administering heavy doses of squid" (19–20).

Péret's imagination leads into regions where rational thinking can follow only at its own risk. How can a dose of squid clean porcelain clay? How heavy a dosage is needed for effective results? None of these questions leads to an answer that reason can accept, and not one of them does imaginative enjoyment treat as relevant. Benjamin Péret's presentation, indeed, is characteristically affirmative, not speculative, paying no tribute to reasonable possibility. This is why the explanations provided in *Histoire naturelle* aggravate the alarm generated in habitual thought.

Among the varieties of petroleum Péret mentions is "granular petroleum that elephants are crazy about because it promotes the growth of their tusks" (19). Is this normal? Well, it all depends upon what we understand by normal—by natural history. Beginning the passage of "Le quatre éléments" devoted to air, Péret declares, "Air, in its normal state, constantly secretes pepper which makes the earth sneeze" (15). At ground level, we are assured, the pepper condenses, giving nonsense in summer and newspaper in winter. All you have to do, it seems, is store the newspaper in a cool place for it to transform itself into a railroad station or a sponge, according to the number of pages it has.

At times, *Histoire naturelle* reads like a mad cookbook. At others, it is more like an old travel book, reporting on sights so strange as to defy belief. The main difference, though, is that world travelers' exotic tales could be authenticated by observation, their reports being verifiable in nature. Péret's account, on the other hand, seeks no authentication outside the realm of the imagination, because it does not admit the necessity for our idea of what really exists to be limited by the visible. And this is why the marvelous universe to which imagination gives access is found to be perpetually self-generative: "Hairy petroleum, which attaches itself to the bark of trees in cold countries and, in the end, successively gives sparrows' eggs, fire crackers, and pins," is a representative example of imaginative creation, since the coupling of the fire crackers and the pins gives birth to red billiard balls that terrify carp: "Their ferocity is such that in a few days the pools best stocked with fish become empty and the billiard ball quickly dies of starvation, producing will o' the wisp" (20).

"Nothing in its place!" This indeed must be our impression of the natural universe, as depicted by Benjamin Péret. For flora does seem to be "condemned to wander from species to species," having to resign itself to "the most singular coupling" (47). "Everything is possible," says the agave, as it promises to extract a zebra from a smoked boat-wash-house and a toad from a flowering thimble, on condition it can work by moonlight so as to separate the toad from a flea (56).

V *"Everything Is Possible"*

Whether precise or vague, the details to be gleaned in *Histoire naturelle* regarding processes of mythical metamorphoses always raise more questions than they answer in the rational mind. Reason finds itself repeatedly at a loss to establish links, firm or even tenuous, between procedure and the results to which it leads. Moreover, rational judgment finds the end product of this process or that entirely devoid of validity. Dried and stored all winter in a dry place, air, for instance, gives an engagement ring the following spring. But this is no ordinary ring, an item marketable in a jewelry store. For one thing, its extreme sensitivity to variations in temperature makes it very fragile. For another, it "rarely attains adult age" (16).

As we reflect upon the absurdity of this product, we see that Péret's ring is unacceptable to the reasoning mind because common sense can assign it no useful function in a world where productivity is meaningful only when its usefulness is immediately perceptible. And so when we notice that the principle of cause and effect, as we are accustomed to its manifestations, is discarded in *Histoire naturelle*, we are really witnessing dislocation of the idea of utilitarianism (what is the advantage of having a ring that has little likelihood of growing up?), radical modification of the generally accepted notion of the functional.

This feature of Benjamin Péret's writing is one to which we shall have occasion to return, when speaking of his verse. It deserves mention at this stage, however, because it enables us to grasp a fundamentally important fact. To enjoy the work of Péret presupposes unforced responsiveness neither to charm, sophistication, naiveté, nor to technical skill, nor even again to a concerted attack upon some supposedly outdated literary convention. Rather, such enjoyment means quite simply a natural disposition to accept the poet's invitation to advance over the threshold of imagination into the marvelous. Flying fire, he tells us, is forbidden in milliners' workrooms, "for it sets working girls against the boss" (26). If sober reflection can explain neither the how nor the why of flying fire's effect on certain working girls—and in fact is brought to a dead stop by the idea that such fire exists at all—this is because questions like these inevitably must lead reasonable thought into an impasse of frustration. Only someone whose own imagination gathers momentum as a result of reading Péret can benefit richly from acquaintance with his work.

In *Histoire naturelle* credibility is not a standard that can be met by conformity to scientific truth or by respect for observable reality. It rests instead upon compatibility of aim in the poet and his audience. Benjamin Péret speaks most clearly and most compellingly to those seeking the same satisfactions as he through a sense of liberation, of freedom earned by imaginative activity, in the face of opposition from natural laws—in which Péret had no faith—or in scientfic conjecture—in which he placed no confidence.

CHAPTER 4

Exploring the Marvelous:
Novel and Stories

I Beyond Realism

THE impression of Benjamin Péret some will gain from
reading André Breton's *Nadja*—that of an inexperienced
provincial, eager to come to the French capital and make a
name for himself in literature, a career even—is misleading on
several counts. In one respect, particularly, this impression calls
for correction without further delay. Unlike Breton and other
friends and acquaintances, Péret did not make a false start by
pursuing literary goals, before feeling the attraction first of
Dada and then of Surrealism. He never found himself faced
with the necessity to repudiate a literary past (one thinks of
Breton's poems inspired by Symbolism, of Tristan Tzara's pre-
Dada poems, of Roger Vitrac's traditional verse collection *Le
Faune noir*), in order to be free to advance through Surrealism
into poetry. No texts survive that allow us to measure any change
brought about in his outlook by association with Dada and
affiliation with Surrealism. And there is reason to believe that
none ever existed.[1] What Benjamin Péret was to be as a writer
he became at once. No evolution is observable in his work, over
a period extending for almost forty years. Moreover, this is as
true of his writings in prose as of those in verse.

Péret's first volume of poems, *Le Passager du transatlantique*,
was published in 1921 in the Collection "Dada." His first published story, *Au 125 du boulevard Saint-Germain*, appeared in
the Collection "Littérature" in 1923. Péret had no call to con-
veniently forget these works, after the appearance of the first
Surrealist manifesto. For each of them testified to the manifestation within Dada of aspirations to which the *Manifeste du*

Surréalisme was to give a name. Each bore witness to the fact that Benjamin Péret did not have to wait until Breton recommended automatic writing, in 1924, before practicing automatism in preference to all other methods of composition. To Péret it was the best method, the only method, first and last. It led him at once beyond realism into the realm of the marvelous.

It is true that, opening his story "Les vagues âmes," written in 1925, we come upon the sentence, "I was alone in a deserted, fetid alley with paving stones missing like the teeth in the jaw of a shrewish old woman." The image that claims our attention here might well suggest to some readers acquainted with French Naturalist novels, and with those inspired by them, that he is on familiar ground. His confidence in this conclusion will be strengthened, no doubt, when, turning to a longer narrative dating from the next year, "... Et les seins mouraient ...,"[2] he encounters the phrase, "we, whose teeth give off the acrid smell of decaying mushrooms." Yet if he went no farther, such a reader would take away a totally erroneous impression of Péret's attitude, as this is to be judged in relation to the realist tradition in literature.

If a rare text subtly evoking the atmosphere of the South American jungle, "La Lumière ou la vie,"[3] has anything to teach us about Benjamin Péret, it is that this was a writer who treated description of the world about him and depiction of the universe to which his imagination gave access as two distinct and quite unconnected activities. Although some might describe "La Lumière ou la vie," rich in suggestive detail and vibrant with sensitivity, as poetic, it stands far apart from poetry, as Péret conceived it. In his creative work, instead of seeking a faithful recreation of the everyday world, in whatever exotic form, and far from concerned to capture the depressing or repulsive aspects of daily life, Péret saw his function as a poet in quite a different light. Much more indicative of his outlook, therefore, are those images that place realistic detail at the service of an antirealistic interpretation of people, facts, and events, the better to disturb our sense of what is real and true: "Ah! sir and dear unknown, whose nose wriggles like a fish caught on a hook ..." ("Ne pas manger de raisin sans le laver"), "Pearls fall periodically from his ears like menstrua" (*La Brebis galante*); "This hour that I can't refrain from comparing to the marriage of a blind girl to a door that closes automatically" ("... Et les seins mouraient..."); "A certain day when the sea will be the color of a thirsty dog"; "he looks at me still sniggering like a rotten tomato"; and—again from "... Et les seins mouraient..."—this more complex example: "Road of algebra where the elephants consecrated by the North Wind knit stockings, I salute you for your length, equaled only by that of Macarelle's hair."

At first, and especially if an isolated example catches our eye as we skim a story of Péret's, comparisons like these appear gratuitous, not to say unacceptable. Further examination of a number of his tales, in which comparisons of this type occur frequently, persuades us that they evidence a consistent approach to the normal, to which Péret's narratives in large measure owe their special tone. In consequence, those images which at first made us imagine ourselves on familiar ground serve after a while only as distant landmarks that allow us to estimate how far we have traveled in Péret's company from the world we habitually treat as real. We soon learn that references to normality come up in Péret's stories only with ironic intent, as is the case in "Il était une boulangère," which he wrote in 1924: "At the moment when they thought to move away from the oak tree (or from Raymond Poincaré, if you prefer), a tomato bobbed up at their feet. That would have been altogether normal, if the tomato hadn't begun breathing like a human being." Thus, whether he is asking us to accept the abnormal just because he tells us it is normal, or emphasizing how distant is what he describes from normality—"all that wasn't normal," he observes pointedly in "Les vagues âmes"—the result is the same. Péret furnishes ample proof of his complete disrespect for the habitual. When in *La Brebis galante* a woman of average height and intelligence goes up to a rock of granite and inquires about its health, the narrator comments, "That didn't surprise me, for I thought of the possibility of the existence of a weasel inside the rock. I'd have been more surprised if I'd seen the same woman go up to a weasel, supposing it had a granite rock in its belly. This proves that there is a distinction to be made between Nestor [the central figure of this novella] and a sewing machine."

Underlying the treatment accorded normality in Péret's stories
is an argument that finds restatement in one of the last of his
texts to appear before his death:

> To demand the subordination of poetry and art to science is a
> deadly aberration, denunciation of which must be sought unceasingly,
> since it consists in overturning the natural order of things, intuition
> coming well ahead of science.
>   ... [Art and poetry] can no more prosper in a scientific climate
> than a fish in the burning sands of the Sahara. Finally both take as
> their authority total liberty, which at the same time they contribute
> to establishing.[4]

The perspective in which Benjamin Péret asks us to view his
short stories is one that offers enjoyment in the form of inversion
of the normal, as we have been accustomed to understand it.
His starting point is that the normal depicted in realistic literature is but the image projected by a distorted view of things,
being posited on the unnatural. In this sense, his stories mark
a readjustment, a rearrangement of the familiar. This is effected
under the guidance not of common sense or the principle of
rationality, but of an intuition that promotes the unlikely, the
inconceivable even, to the status of normality and does so to
the detriment of realist principles, now condemned as outmoded.

II The Reeducation of Mental Sight

Jean-Louis Bédouin has characterized reading the short stories
of Benjamin Péret as "an indispensable exercise in the re-
education of mental sight" (72). This exercise can weaken trust
in familiar reality as immutable and always fully satisfying to
man. And it warns us to beware of logic, if we persist in relying
upon habitual processes of perception to reassure us about the
stability of the world in which we feel at ease. More exactly,
Péret's tales allow us to see that his refusal to separate reason
from unreason, on the theoretical plane, went with an incapacity,
during the creative process, to respect the "artificial opposition"
between poetic thought and logical thought.
  Pursuing to a logical conclusion situations and actions that

take their origin outside the normal, Péret puts the principle of logic in question. In "Au 125 du boulevard Saint-Germain" one of his characters pushes open an apartment door, is greeted by the smell of hay, and finds, naturally, that the room is occupied by a freshly watered, newly mown lawn. When, in ". . . Et les seins mouraient . . . ," someone mentions the word "France," the consequence is immediate and apparently inevitable: "It is probable," we are told, "that the mere word 'France' had the power to create mother-of-pearl, for scarcely had he pronounced this word than all the absurd everyday objects that populated Macarelle's drawing room became covered in mother-of-pearl, like a dead tree with moss, to the astonishment of all present." This one-sentence paragraph brings together elements typical of Péret's handling of the short story. While those present at the scene described are astonished by it, the narrator remains imperturbable. Objects belonging to familiar experience are merely absurd at first. Describing their transformation, Péret proceeds to borrow from observable reality a comparison that will fix in our minds a picture without precedent in the world we have known up to now.

The ironic effect created in circumstances such as these may be increased, of course, by the narrator's assurance of the veracity of his tale, or again it may happen that he insists upon the ludicrous character of something taking place. Either way, particular emphasis is likely to come from his use of a notably unliterary familiar style. For the language we find in Péret's stories is consistent with his indifference to introducing a narrator who is a literary persona, recognizable to all by an authorial voice that can be identified without difficulty. On occasion, the narrator seems, understandably, a creation of verbal automatism and, as such, a strange figure among other strange characters. At other times, however, he appears to stand apart from the participants, as though his origin were different from theirs, and he functions as a witness to the revelations of automatism. Thus the narrator is capable of shifting position disconcertingly, vis à vis the subject matter of his tale. Sometimes he speaks from close up, authoritatively affirming that the inconceivable is indeed true, perhaps. Sometimes, though, he stands back from events, either expressing his surprise and soliciting ours, or surprising us by his calm acceptance of the improbable or the impossible.

Benjamin Péret writes stories as if he has before him someone to whom he can address himself directly and without affectation. An air of intimacy between narrator and reader thus gives special prominence to the former's frequent interjections, some conversational, some ironically literary in tone: "Alas!" "If I may say so," "Oh amazement," "by God," and "but what had happened?" The interesting thing is that time after time we are obliged to conclude that such asides are present not so much to explain or excuse the introduction of unprecedented phenomena or events but to draw attention to the absence of any rational explanation for these, and to Péret's total indifference to supplying any. "Heavens! where is he?" asks the narrator of *La Brebis galante* when Nestor finds himself in Louis XVI's bedchamber, where a golden palm tree is sleeping.

In Péret's writings the tone is never placatory, the mood never conciliatory. The narrator's role is not to offer himself as an intermediary who, having first gained our trust, then entices us into strange territory where we would decline to venture unaccompanied. Instead, he challenges us to advance, without nostalgia for what is behind us, into a world of unprecedented situations and encounters. "Put yourself in their place," he tells us in "Ne pas manger de raisin sans le laver." "Do I have to tell you that . . . ?" he asks in *La Brebis galante*. In both cases, he is bringing to our notice disturbing details typical of the irrationality that pervades his narrative universe, where the principle of causality is recurrently disrupted.

Bowing to that principle would be inconsistent with the efficient exploration of a world that is Péret's own, because it has been freed of dependence upon cause and effect, as reasonable experience teaches us to believe in their interconnection. Thus, far more than the mere dislocation of language, it is the dislocation of ideas that Péret offers in *La Brebis galante* and *Le Gigot, sa vie et son œuvre*. As a consequence, the intimacy created by the narrative mode in all the stories he relates—even in "La dernière nuit d'un condamné à mort" which tells how Benjamin Péret went to the guillotine—is not, and cannot be, a source of comfort to those who find them strange and even alarming. On the contrary, the effect is anything but reassuring when, in "Il était une boulangère," the narrator, speaking of one character—Pope Pius VII, as it happens—asks, "Could he know that in this country the air was heavier than in all the countries he knew? No, don't you agree?"

Regularly we face events that would be beyond belief in the everyday world. When this happens, for the most part Péret's characters meet the situation without surprise. Or, like the central figure in his "Une Vie pleine d'intérêt," they readily find an explanation, satisfying to them if not to the reasonable mind:

Coming out of her house early in the morning, as usual, Mrs. Lannor saw that her cherry trees, still covered with fine red fruit the day before, had been replaced during the night by stuffed giraffes. A silly joke! Why did Mrs. Lannor think to accuse a couple of lovers who, the evening before, at nightfall, had come to sit at the foot of one of those trees? To leave there a souvenir of their love, they had engraved their entwined initials in the bark. But Mrs. Lannor had spotted them, and, seizing a sucking pig, she had thrown it at the couple, shouting, "What are you doing there, you artichoke children! Would you like a begonia, by any chance?"

As for the reader, whether he will agree or disagree does not trouble Péret's narrator, who is quite likely to invite speculation just so as to prove it unfounded, as for instance in "Dans le cadre de nos mœurs" ("Within the Framework of our Mores" [1923]):

A car arrived and Bolo Pacha got out. What do you think happened? . . . That Bolo Pacha got on the horse and that, digging in his spurs, he vanished? . . .
Not at all!
Bolo Pacha got down on his knees and holding on to the horse's tail said, "Our Father which art in heaven, etc. . . . ."

It is as if the narrator's aim were to mock our credulity, as in a story called "La Fleur de Napoléon" (1922) reminiscent at this point of the poem "Mémoires de Benjamin Péret": "Out of uniformity is born boredom, out of boredom reflection, out of reflection disgust with life, out of disgust with life artichokes, out of artichokes cows, out of cows children, out of children Napoleon, but you can see very well that I'm saying this for a joke."

Péret speaks jestingly neither as an excuse for what he has told us nor with the purpose of freeing his readers of the necessity to take him seriously. In fact, humor is everywhere a catalytic agent in his writing, both in his prose and in his verse—the element that more persistently perhaps than any other, and more aggressively, marks resistance to the rationalist view of life and of the physical universe.

The form of humor we encounter everywhere in the work of Benjamin Péret is that advocated in Surrealism and described by Marko Ristic in a Yugoslav Surrealist magazine as "the disinterested and direct expression of the unconscious."[5] Humor that warrants use of the adjectives selected by Ristic is in its very essence spontaneous. Hence the special value of automatism in ensuring it an outlet. For, as Ristic phrased it, humor is "in its essence an intuitive and implicit criticism of the conventional mental mechanism." We are not dealing, then, with a technique, with a method carefully applied so as to bring about certain pre-established, well-formulated ends. Rather, humor in Surrealism, and especially in Benjamin Péret's work, is expressive of something we have heard him call poetic intuition: intuition working in a natural, unforced manner to bring about dislocation of the familiar sequence of facts and events and their removal from the so-called normal context of experience. And so, Ristic points out, intuition precipitates them into a "vertiginous play of unexpected surreal relationships."

Nowhere better than in the stories left us by Benjamin Péret does one witness humor, "in contact with poetry," as Ristic stresses, become the "extreme expression of a convulsive irreconciliation, of a revolt to which restraint and repression only give more strength." Everything in Péret's imagined universe, animated at all times by poetic intuition, combats a complacency regarding the everyday world that the narrator must risk finding in his readers. The celebration of the destructive rite of irreconciliation is an exhilarating experience of gathering momentum, as we are shown people, animals, and things multiplying, subdividing, growing extra limbs, or simply coming to meet us in outlandish attire: "Dressed in a swing, the man with hoar-frost eyes was coming forward through the valley," we read in "... Et les seins mouraient. ..." When we first meet Nestor, in *La Brebis galante*, he is wearing a fur-lined coat of banana-tree skin and leading a goat that wears a top hat "with the greatest distinction." Without warning or excuse, the most unexpected phenomena rise before us, like the "procession of monsters with ventilator eyes that advances with the slowness appropriate to their majesty," in "Ne pas manger de raisin sans le laver."

Like the one just cited, sentences have a way of inexorably leading forward, according to their own logic, taking us farther and farther from our preconceptions. Thus, a procession of ventilator-eyed monsters advances slowly because speed would not be appropriate to the majesty of these creatures. To the rational mind, the path we follow in Péret's company is a dangerously slippery one. To those able to respond without reservation to the wonders he brings to our notice, the rewards are rich. They soon learn to be suspicious of the most banal objects. A Louis XV clock can become "ridiculous." So can a certain "public square," despite—or perhaps because of—the grass that, escaping from between its paving stones, rises as high as the houses flanking it.

Persistently Benjamin Péret's descriptive method disregards the criteria upon which the stability of habitual reality rests. We learn to be wary when he refers, for example, to a "wretched plate": the plate in question is made of rhinoceros horns and feathers. Similarly, his narrative approach ushers in the improbable by way of the commonplace. "He sighed. He sighed for such a long time that his feet became blue like a pick wielded by a tall man demolishing a famous church." Overstatement and understatement stand side by side bewilderingly on the printed page, and the reader is left wondering about the "unmentionable purpose" that prompted someone in "Ne pas manger de raisin sans le laver" to cultivate telegraph poles—an activity, we are assured, that has brought him no luck.

III   *Panic Joy Returns*

Noting that Benjamin Péret endows the objects, people, and strange creatures that inhabit the world he has created with "singular mobility and properties that are, to say the least, unexpected," Jean-Christophe Bailly rightly insists that the total freedom of movement conferred upon them "breaks with the dogma of immobility upon which the old world rests" (64). André Breton comments more succinctly in his *Anthologie de l'Humour noir*, when remarking apropos of Péret's work, "Panic joy has returned" (506).

For Péret, investigating the marvelous that opens up beyond the confines of mundane reality was a joyous experience. Embarking upon it, he gladly surrendered respect for the retarding influences from which automatism brings release. As nothing less than unquestioning acceptance is required of those who enter the realm of the marvelous, his stories begin without preamble (unless it be a preamble of doubtful relevance, reasonably speaking). By the time they commence, it is already too late for us to expect commonsense objections to be heeded: "A pistol shot gave the signal to begin, and a blonde lady rose vertically in the air, then slipped lightly over a few clumps of trees, easily crossed a river, and came to rest as simply as can be at the foot of a syringa in blossom." This opening—to a tale entitled, against reason, "Une Ornière vaut une jument" ("A Rut's as Good as a Mare" [1923])—is quite representative. To the protest that one cannot begin a story that way, Paul Eluard replies, in an essay on Péret, "Imagination does not have an instinct for imitation. It is the spring and the flood that no boat can go against."[6] Objections are meaningless, when they rest upon the assumption—which Surrealists see as false—that the task facing imagination is the recreation of the familiar, rather than probing the marvelous.

The use of adverbs at the beginning of "Une Ornière vaut une jument," to equate the abnormal with the normal, is characteristic of the manner in which Péret unhesitatingly reconciles reality and imagination in that marvelous amalgam called the Surreal. When in "Une Vie pleine d'intérêt" ("A Life Full of Interest" [1922]) Mrs. Lannor finds herself among a multitude of sardines, these stand on their tails and greet her "politely." In "Les Malheurs d'un dollar" (1922), the single tooth in Mr. Détour's jaw "replaces a watch to advantage." Hector, we learn, is in "Ne pas manger de raisin sans le laver" "generally the grandfather because he is watching the fleas jumping over the river of grandstands." "Les vagues âmes" mentions a boa constrictor that "bowed ceremoniously to us, which for a boa consists, as everyone knows, in wrapping itself around the right foot of the person being greeted."

We witness here something André Breton once called "the only *evidence* in the world," tracing it to "the spontaneous, extralucid, insolent relationship established in certain conditions between this and that, which common sense would hold us back from bringing face to face." Here then is a clue to Breton's deep admiration for Péret: "Just as the most hateful word seems to me to be the word *therefore*, with all it entails by way of vanity and morose delectation, so I love to distraction that which, breaking at random the thread of discursive thought, suddenly goes off like a rocket, illuminating a life of relationships fruitful in a new way, to which everything indicates that men in earliest times held the secret."[7]

Nothing can be gained from posing reasonable questions, which Péret's calm indifference indicates to be irrelevant: "A boa in the streets of Paris at this hour! what on earth can that mean?" asks Pius VII, without the least hope of receiving a reply. Experience teaches us that, so far as Péret is concerned, anything can happen, if only the moment is propitious. And all that is needed, really, is something Benjamin Péret possessed to an unparalleled degree—the ability to resist, in practice, the "extravagant overestimation of the known compared with what remains to be known," against which André Breton protested in theory.[8] "That morning," begins "La Fleur de Napoléon," "little orange-colored fish were moving about through the atmosphere." On a day mentioned in "... Et les seins mouraient...," the streets of the French capital are strewn with "skeletons of antediluvian animals, electrical appliances, and out-of-fashion women's dresses." The tale called "Au 125 du boulevard Saint-Germain" begins at 11:30 at night: "a few taxis were passing nonchalantly and the dromedaries had not all gone home." Nicolas Calas' comment is pertinent: "To *responsibility* the surrealists oppose *revelation*. From *inspiration to revelation* and from there again to further inspiration! These are the units in the *rhythmical movement* of the poet's life. The result is *marvelous* (as opposed to *mysterious*)."[9]

Péret contests the stability of the familiar world, reasonably conceived, through his attack upon the fixity of objects, limited and classified in function. Liberating these for his own use, he questions much more than the laws of custom and habit by which reason denies objects in the material world mobility and autonomy of action. For it is the way people and things lend themselves to poetic use that fascinates Péret. In his poetic universe the center of gravity shifts away from rationality. Hence one's first impression may be that what we see here is unacceptably unreasonable. But the poetic experience is for Péret essentially a liberative one. It brings about liberation from situations and ideas we have known for too long to find satisfying any more. And, more important, it frees us for unprecedented experiences upon which familiarity has not laid its patina of disappointment. Perhaps, then, the most distinctive feature of Péret's poetic endeavor, in prose no less than in verse, is not so much what it makes us see as what it encourages us to be willing to see. Péret's is a world in perpetual creation. From the moment when the writer takes up his pen, everything is refreshingly available, capable of taking on new and unforeseen life. Here no concession can be made to the memories readers may bring with them from the world upon which the narrator has turned his back. Péret prefers to speak directly to an audience with whom no compromise is necessary. From the beginning—and it is noteworthy that almost all of his stories were written during the twenties, a considerable number of them antedating the 1924 *Manifesto of Surrealism*—he made no effort to accommodate his public's preconceptions, to entice or cajole. His work bespeaks total lack of concern for those who need to be persuaded to the Surrealist viewpoint. From the outset, Péret wrote in such a manner as to exclude readers of this kind.

The imagery that lends distinction to Péret's writings resists the categories and classifications of our ordered world. It substitutes for these other classifications that are no less consistent in his imagined universe than are ours in the world with which we are familiar. What counts here is not childlike acceptance, uncritically granted,[10] but responsiveness to the story-teller's function as a manipulator of people, events, and even natural phenomena: Péret was far more literally sole owner and proprietor of the world he created than William Faulkner was of Yoknapatawpha County. Péret's custom of mingling, against the background of Paris, the habitual (the taxis in "Au 125 du boulevard Saint-Germain") with the unfamiliar (the dromedaries, not *all* of which have returned home by 11:30 at night) places the unexpected and even the improbable on an equal footing with the familiar, which usually goes unquestioned. In this way, we cannot successfully challenge the existence of the one without casting doubt on the other, any more than we are free to believe in the one while ignoring the other.

IV   *"The Eternal Resources of the Spirit"*

In a note on the Surrealist painter Wifredo Lam, Péret once spoke of expressing "those eternal resources of the spirit that, in every language and every tone, speaks in turn of desire and of terror."[11] What commands Péret's attention in his short stories is not the fantastic, which clashes with the real, and not simply the mysterious which, ahead of Calas, André Breton condemned,[12] but the "heart and nervous system of all poetry," the marvelous.

Péret's love of the marvelous marks an aspiration to establish new equivalences between the observed and the imaginary, set at a new level of perception and understanding which is the Surreal. In this, his fidelity to Surrealist principles is exemplary. Surrealism does not seek to overthrow one form of reality and replace it with another. Being a heightened sense of what is real, Surrealism makes it necessary for us to detect in the reality we face from day to day a potential source of pleasure to which we have remained insensitive. As Breton intimates in his *Anthologie de l'Humour noir*, reaching out for the marvelous means, in part, practicing a form of humor that is "par excellence the mortal enemy of sentimentality" as well as of "short-term fancy" (21–22). And so Péret's work bears comparison to a significant degree with that of Sade, described in Breton's anthology as "ground that lends itself to a mutation of life" (64). Mutant forms—animal and natural— are not merely fanciful adornments; rather, they bear witness to the resistance offered the reality principle by another, namely, the pleasure principle of which Sigmund Freud spoke.

It would be contrary to Péret's purpose to dismiss the known in favor of a fanciful world quite arbitrarily substituted for it. Thus the nonsense we meet in his writings accords with that defined by Robert Benayoun as "the far-fetched detours of disappointment of the critical mind."[13] To Benjamin Péret, the immanence of the Surreal is a demonstrable fact, whereas the observable universe of accepted relationships serves only to furnish the artist with the occasion to uncover its Surrealist virtualities and bring them to full development. And so the taxis of "Au 125 du boulevard Saint-Germain" are as necessary as the dromedaries, when it comes to preparing us for our meeting with the principal personages of this early tale: the King of Greece and the President of the Republic, resplendent in a diving suit.

The manner in which Péret disposes of the disparity in the so-called normal world between the familiar and the unthought-of is a distinctive feature of his narrative approach. In "Au 125 du boulevard Saint-Germain," for instance, we find that when the King of Greece follows a strange man, pushing a chair on castors along the Rue Danton, past the Boulevard Saint-Germain, and then up the Seine as far as the Jardin des Plantes, "the trail left by the armchair, that remained, we know not why, luminous, guided him as surely as if he had the ludicrous rig ahead of him." It is entirely characteristic of Benjamin Péret that, declining to explain the reasons for the trail left by the chair, and calling the curious vehicle a "ludicrous rig," he seems to gain our confidence, while at the same time sharpening our sense of the marvelous. As he renders an account of what his imagination has revealed, Péret betrays no proprietary impulse. So it is the detachment he evidences, instead, that serves to authenticate the incredible sights and events animating his stories.

Occasionally, it is true, Benjamin Péret affects the first-person narrative form, as he does in "Un Plaisir bien passager" (1924) and La Brebis galante. But the things he shows us when this happens are no less foreign to everyday experience than in tales where authority for what is related rests with an unidentifiable witness. What is more, an account delivered by someone implicated in events can be just as unacceptable on the level of reason, to judge by "Un Plaisir bien passager," if not more frustrating to reason. The last three paragraphs of this story leave us keenly aware of the absence of an explanation for what has occurred:

A few minutes later, I found myself sitting on a bench on the Boulevard Sébastopol with, by my side, the prettiest young woman imaginable, dressed only in her stockings and a transparent chemise. This occasioned cries and sighs that in the end excited the infrequent passers-by. Then people paired off, and here, there, and everywhere cries testified to what everyone was feeling at that moment.

Suddenly there was a loud noise of horses and weapons and, above the houses, in the dazzling sunshine, famous Napoleonic regiments could be seen marching past, led by military bands.

After they had gone by, all movement ceased. Near the Rue Turbigo, only three sheep were grazing on sparse grass coming up between the shining paving stones.

It would be a mistake to anticipate a desire on Péret's part to persuade, when he makes it clear that he regards persuasion as unnecessary. Hence his use of aggressive assertion, accompanying statements patently unsupported by any evidence beyond that to be found in his fertile imagination. Mentioning Chinese lanterns, the narrator of *La Brebis galante* comments, "Needless to say that, for the occasion, the latter had been extinguished and that their smoke filled the atmosphere with an execrable smell of filthy jesuit." Later he speaks of "the slap I'll give the first person who comes to tell me that these lines don't correspond very exactly to the truth." In "Les Malheurs d'un dollar" we read, "One afternoon then he was finishing emptying a fairly deep pond measuring more than two-and-a-half acres across when, from out of the mud arose, do you hear me, arose a gigantic derby hat which, after attaining a height of nine feet, turned over and dropped into the mud a charming young girl, blonde and pink."

A similar passage occurs in "... Et les seins mouraient...": "But Macarelle knows nothing about his hair. It belongs to the future; he is awaiting it like a love letter and sometimes when the rain is falling on the plain after the fashion of a child who has leaned imprudently out of a sixth-floor window, he eats it. That surprises you? HE EATS IT! And why couldn't he eat his hair?" At no time does the uncompromising nature of Péret's iconoclastic attitude to conventional reality show to better advantage than when, for instance, he insists in the same story that a burning bundle of straw seems to swim: "Don't think that 'swims' is more or less what I mean. . . ." No mental reservations are tolerated, no hesitation is permissible. If it were otherwise, how could the reader interest himself in the affairs of the unconventional people who move so purposefully through Péret's universe?

A door opened and a voice with a Meridional accent said, rolling the r, "What is it, my good sir?"

"I should like to see Mr. Seraphin, you know, the gentleman who throws bathtubs out of the window at half-past eleven."

"Fourth floor, on the right," said the voice. ("Au 125 du boulevard Saint-Germain")

Although we may wonder whether, if we finally do encounter the strange Mr. Seraphin, we will ever learn why he hurls bathtubs into the street late at night, it is imperative that we do not doubt for a moment that he really exists. If we do not believe in him as completely as the President of the Republic does, when knocking at his door, then how can we appreciate the President's joy when, at the end of his quest, he and Mr. Seraphin meet face to face?

This question will appear specious unless we realize that all of Benjamin Péret's short stories vindicate the rights of the imagination, in the face of the constrictions that rational thinking generally imposes upon human desire. This is to say that the stories left us by Péret are expressions of desire. And desire, he insisted, resides in the unconscious. It was desire that he had in view when he spoke in *La Parole est à Péret* of man dominating the world more and more with a mind "freed of all impediments." Casting reason down from its "celestial throne" means, in the world of Péret's poetic stories, acknowledging the prior claim of desire over that form of reality to which his essay "La Pensée est UNE et indivisible" referred as "the rational product of absurd and horrible social restraint."

"What use is it to you to be a man," a horse asks the Cuirassier de Richshoffen in "...Et les seins mouraient...," "if you can't change lead into cork and cork into lead?" The narrative supplies no answer, to be sure. But we need have no hesitation in concluding what response Péret invites us to formulate. His stories stand as proof of an attitude in which he placed unreserved confidence. Throughout his life, Benjamin Péret had in view a reply to this fundamental question, in which total trust goes not to mystery—that exceeds man's comprehension—but to the marvelous, the very image of man's affranchisement from the oppressive forces Péret felt it essential to resist. "Poetry," he wrote in *VVV*'s fourth number, "is elsewhere, feverishly wielding the indispensable guillotine." And so Péret instinctively placed his stories in that *somewhere else* which he situated in the realm of the marvelous, where reason and unreason are no longer in conflict but united on a plane of perception and response which mundane reality conceals from sight.

Resorting to automatism, as he did so naturally, Péret exercised no conscious control over the content of his stories. Hence, so far as they embody features testifying to the intrusion of the marvelous into human experience, they do so under the influence of intuition, not theoretical argument.[14] As Péret had occasion to discover, after his imprisonment in Rennes, the marvelous may reveal itself, but it can be neither conjured up nor summoned at will. His tales were not written expressly to satisfy humanity's "thirst for the irrational," but simply in response to a thirst he himself felt. And so, when he placed logic at the service of irrationality, he did not do so because he proposed to mount an attack upon the irrational, but because automatism had released him from acceptance of an "artificial opposition" which, on the theoretical plane, he declined to condone in *La Parole est à Péret.*

"And his arm flew off to reach the horizon which it pierced like an arrow passing through to the other side of an eye" ("La Maladie N° 9"). Total imaginative freedom permits of irrational development in stories by Benjamin Péret that, while never limited by the world in which we are accustomed to live, never leave it so far behind that we forget its existence. In drawing us out of habitual thought processes, liberating aspects of reality we regarded as forever fixed, Péret exercises a form of poetic intuition that, with reasonable reservations now cast aside, he identifies with the essence of poetry, the marvelous. In consequence, his tales permit us to "pass through to the other side of an eye," to where the marvelous reigns. And the same is true of his *Mort aux Vaches et au champ d'honneur.*

Benjamin Péret did not affix the subtitle "novel" to his *Mort aux Vaches*, written before André Breton roundly attacked the novel form in his 1924 Surrealist manifesto. Given the Surrealists' contempt for literary genres, there is no good reason why he should have done so. Nevertheless Péret did identify each section of his book under titled chapter headings, numbered consecutively. Externally, at all events, *Mort aux Vaches* is invested with the appearance of a novel. Opening it, we expect to find a unified narrative, purposefully structured. Yet acquaintance with the text leaves us no alternative but to conclude that the author's purpose was entirely ironical, so far as respect for the novel form is concerned.

It is not only that, halfway through, the narrator confesses to having written his story from inside an enormous pebble, nine feet high. For we have no assurance that, in *Mort aux Vaches*, it is always the same voice that we hear relating events. The longer we read, the more insistently this book demands that we revise our ideas about the form and function of narrative and acknowledge the need for entertaining new answers to the old questions: what has the writer to communicate, and how is communication to be effected?

A noteworthy, disconcerting feature of this curious work is that it consists of automatic texts interspersed with sections obviously quite deliberately fashioned—an absurd debate in the Chamber of Deputies, a succession of unrelated letters, a whole chapter written in footnoted slang—which evidence no greater cohesion and sense of narrative purpose than do the fruits of automatism. By means somewhat different, then, *Mort aux Vaches* gives the same impression as *La Brebis galante.* In the latter, where frequent metamorphoses come to our attention, the narrative often changes form as well as direction. In *Mort aux Vaches*, too, instead of the text taking on responsibility for developing plot, the latter is swallowed up by the text, submerged to the point where it cannot be salvaged, let alone summarized, and disappearing without any sign of concern or regret on the narrator's part.

Indeed, Péret's treatment of novelistic form is characteristically Surrealist. If it differs from what one encounters in Desnos' *La Liberté ou l'amour!* or Crevel's *Babylone*, it is only to the extent that Péret's approach to the novel is even more disrespectful than his fellow Surrealists'. A foundering genre is scuttled, while all that remains is what really interests the writer: an accumulation of marvels, strung together without his bothering to pay lip service to the conventions of the novel such as we still find in Roussel's *Impressions d'Afrique* and *Locus Solus*, which offer perhaps the closest parallel to *Mort aux Vaches et au champ d'honneur*.

The kind of enjoyment Péret's pseudonovel has to offer is similar to that brought us by his short stories. A fishing boat comes upon a flower bed with a young baby on it, guarded by a tricolor fly:

> The captain ordered them to tie up the flower bed to the boat and take the infant and its baby-sitter on board. With a gaffe, a sailor tried to detain the flower bed as it drifted by. No sooner had his gaffe touched the flower bed when an immense clock spring shot out of the corolla of a flower, entwined at mad speed around the gaffe and, continuing in its reckless path, penetrated the sailor's right eye only to emerge at once through his navel. A moment later, the sailor had disappeared and the gaffe stood still in space, its hook just touching the flower bed. In place of the sailor there was now only a chocolate nun. (11)

Since the advantages of the novel form, as Péret chose to make use of it, did not outweigh those of the short story, it is not surprising that *Mort aux Vaches et au champ d'honneur* stands alone in his work. The sustained format of the novel, however abused, is not so conducive to maintenance of the kind of poetic intensity that Péret discovered in automatism. His imaginative qualities found the short story better suited to their expression, especially during the twenties. In the long run, however, it was verse that provided Benjamin Péret with the most natural framework for poetry.

CHAPTER 5

Mechanics of the Marvelous
I: Conjunctions

I *Casting Down the Barriers of Stupidity and Routine*

ATTEMPTING to uncover the mechanics of the marvelous in the writings of Benjamin Péret carries some risks. So accustomed are we to reading poets whose work images their intentions, that the presence of identifiable characteristics in Péret's poetic handling of reality lends itself quite naturally to interpretation as evidence of a concerted plan for dealing with reality, supposedly kept always in sight during the process of composition.[1] Yet such a deliberate approach would be totally inconsistent with the undisciplined flow of verbal automatism, so leading to the conclusion that Péret was by no means as genuine an automatist as Surrealists have claimed. Alternatively, it might appear that he felt entitled to treat automatic writing as no more than the first stage in poetic composition, to be succeeded by editorial revision, development of this or that effect, addition of this detail or that.

In reality, of course, Péret's conception of the role of automatism differed radically from that of Paul Eluard, who looked upon automatic writing as merely increasing, developing, and enriching the "field of poetic consciousness."[2] Hence analysis of his tales yields no technique for short-story telling that others might hope to borrow for their own purposes. Instead it provides ample evidence that the automatic method led the author of *Le Gigot, sa vie et son œuvre* to externalize a peculiar view of reality that reflected no conscious effort to manipulate evidence drawn from the material world about him, and yet was so distinctive in character as to be unmistakably that of Benjamin Péret. This is why a similar examination of the ways in which dedication to the marvelous influenced the form of his verse

74

helps lead us farther into the universe which Péret explored throughout four decades of poetic activity.

When we take up Péret's verse, there is no advantage in searching for technical devices that presumably might lend themselves to adoption, adaptation, or parody. More to the point by far is being alert to signs recurrently expressive of the manner in which Péret's imagination made connections between one event and the next, between one phenomenon and another, as it advanced through successive stages of poetic intuition. Rather than try to demonstrate how the poet apparently aims to affect our sensibility, let us concern ourselves, so much more appropriately, with how his verse takes its effect, in conducting us into the world of the marvelous.

This is not an approach of convenience, as such rightly open to suspicion. On the contrary, it is a way of attempting without prejudice to become acquainted with Péret's verse, an approach that the very nature of his poetry recommends. For not the least disconcerting aspect of a poem by Benjamin Péret is this: it seems to proceed by non sequiturs instead of advancing according to a readily perceptible plan, an organized structure that gives us confidence to follow where the poet leads. A *disjunctive* principle seems in operation almost everywhere. Thus, one often hesitates to refer to the development of a theme, or even to speak of a succession of meaningfully arranged images. Even readers who believe that they come to Péret's work with a completely open mind may soon have the feeling of being shut out by a poet who apparently cares not at all how readily he communicates with his public.

The disruptive principle underlying Péret's writing is epitomized in his remarkable imagery. The latter betokens such a radical departure from poetic precedent that it may well command the reader's exclusive—and puzzled—attention. To be able to go forward into Péret's poetic universe, though, and to be able to assimilate the images that give flavor to his writing, we have to learn how to respond to a distinctive grammatical structure that provides his verse with its characteristic framework. Examination of that framework offers insights into Péret's poetic concepts and their application. Consideration of a single feature of grammatical structure, the conjunction, is enough to

reveal how conjunctive elements paradoxically appear to serve
the disjunctive principle in Péret's poems, so helping to "level
the barriers raised time after time by stupidity and routine."

II *"Because"*

Normally the conjunction serves to unite sense as well as
structure. Its designated grammatical role is not simply to join
but also to impose upon the elements it brings together a link
that makes unquestionable sense of their proximity. Underlying
the conventional use of conjunctions, therefore, we can detect
certain rational suppositions regarding the manner and the
nature of verbal exchange. These, needless to say, are assump-
tions that the poems of Benjamin Péret challenge violently
and at every turn.

It is really of no account that conjunctions of the type
that interest us are absent altogether from Péret's first volume
of verse, *Le Passager du transatlantique*. It matters no more
that their presence is not equally noticeable from collection
to collection, after 1921. For it is clear that poems grouped
under one title tend to fall more readily into structural forms
that dispense with conjunctions than others do. What is important is not so much how frequently conjunctions occur in Péret's
writings as the forceful way our attention is drawn by their use
to the manner in which his poetic imagination typically operated.

It is no easy matter to select verses illustrative of Péret's
handling of conjunctions that will allow us to move forward
from simple examples to more complex ones. Of course, it is
not hard to pick out lines that are quite elementary, on the
plane of verbal structure; the following are examples:

> les chats bondissent parce que leur queue s'envole

> the cats bound because their tails are flying off

> > (*Un Point c'est tout* [1946] II, 185)[3]

> Mais la tempête ment comme une soupe

> But the storm tells lies like a soup

> > (*Immortelle Maladie* [1924] I, 63)

However, the question of relative simplicity or complexity can be neither posed nor answered in relation to linguistic sophistication alone. What makes them more or less difficult to deal with is the fact that conjunctions of the kind represented here have a special value. The explanatory role reserved for them in conventional usage is subverted in the antirational realm to which Péret's poetry is the pathway. Here phenomena that reason finds unjustifiable exist side by side, or even engender one another. Functioning normally, conjunctions would be at odds with poetry, as Péret was dedicated to its practice.

Determinedly opposed to a view of reality based on rational supposition, Péret could only have betrayed the cause to which he was committed, had he allowed conjunctions to impose constraints upon imaginative invention. It was only natural, then, that, according to the logic of poetry which topples reason, conjunctions should find themselves in Péret's verse contributing to reclaiming the world from an illusory sense of dependence upon rational premises. Conjunctions regularly mark a lyrical departure from the mundane, undertaken in the interest of imaginative freedom. They become liberating agents since, through their use, Péret denies the reasoning mind the reassurance of finding his poetic statement totally incoherent while, like the English Gothic novel, his poem "extracts the marvelous, quivering with passion, from the far end of the attic to which rationalist thought had relegated it."[4]

If, to begin with, we confine our attention to the conjunction "because," we find it used in a manner that overturns the principle of cause and effect, as this is generally understood and applied in our reasonable world. The effect is to set causal sequence on a new track and to discredit predictability, from which routine is born:

Et personne ne passera plus sur la route parce que les lettres seront des mitrailleuses hystériques.

And no one will be able to use the road any more because letters will be hysterical machine guns.

(*Le Grand Jeu* [1928] I, 121)

Utilized in this fashion, "because" repudiates its traditional role—the role for which it was enlisted by reason. Hence its effect is no longer to enclose the poetic statement within the zone of familiar, habitual reality, but to open upon the unfamiliar and the unforeseen. Instead of being a fence to keep out the marvelous, the conjunction promises to be a window upon it.

This, then, is why Péret's writings do not shirk explanations but rather abound in them. The explanations provided, instead of confining imaginative flights to the restricted atmosphere of reasonable acceptance, take us far beyond its limitations, frequently rivaling the strange sights and events they are called upon to justify, or even exceeding these in strangeness. In one text, for instance, a long passage incorporates the following prediction which reminds us that Surrealism reserves a prophetic role for poetry:

> Les grands arbres seront morts
> et les seins suspendus à leurs branches
> se soulèveront régulièrement pour signifier leur sommeil

> The big trees will be dead
> and the breasts suspended from their branches
> will rise regularly to signify their sleep

And why should this be so? Responding to our need to understand, Péret's explanation brooks no objection from reason, which prompts us to seek to comprehend:

> Tout cela tout cela parce qu'un chien court après sa queue
> et ne la retrouve pas
> parce que les pavés sont sortis en rangs
>   pressés et menacent les rivières
> parce que les plantes dépérissent dans des
>   scaphandres désaffectés
> parce que l'eau ne s'égoutte plus entre les doigts
> tout cela enfin parce que tu n'es plus qu'une figurine
> découpée dans un billet de banque

> All because all because a dog is chasing his tail
> and can't find it
> because the paving stones are out in serried ranks
>   and threaten the rivers

because the plants are withering away in
                                        disused diving suits
because water no longer drips between fingers
all because finally you are no longer anything but a figurine
cut out of a bank note

(Le Grand Jeu I, 137–38)

Our feeling of disorientation is increased, not diminished, as Péret prolongs his explanation in a manner that profits from ambiguity. It is disconcerting enough to find him combining a number of improbable circumstances to account for the situation his poem forecasts. But is it not even more difficult for reasonable thought to cope with the possibility that Péret's first explanatory clause may depend upon the second, which in turn rests upon the third, while the third is itself the consequence of the fourth? However we interpret what Péret has written, it is clear that he grants the word "because" a pivotal position in his poetic statement, where its function is never in doubt: it supplies an explanation that heightens the antirational effect of the poem as a whole—when we would anticipate that it must reduce or control it—so enriching the lyrical content of his text:

Et je vous attends avec le sel des spectres
dans les reflets des eaux volages
dans les malheurs des acacias
dans le silence des fentes
précieuses entre toutes parce qu'elles vous ont souri
comme sourient les nuages aux miracles
comme sourient les liquides aux enfants
comme sourient les traits aux points

And I await you with the salt of ghosts
in the reflections of fickle waters
in the misfortunes of acacias
in the silence of cracks
precious above all because they have smiled at you
as the clouds smile at miracles
as liquids smile at children
as dashes smile at dots

(Immortelle Maladie I, 61)

III *Also "for"*

Like "because," in the poems of Benjamin Péret the conjunction "for" is a trap set to snare the unwary into looking for a logic that the poet long since has put aside. Thus, in the lines below, one is at a loss to find a necessary connection, satisfying to common sense, between what precedes "for" and what follows it:

Si je vais sur l'océan je charmerai tous les poissons et les pêcheurs me maudiront car les poissons seront centenaires pour avoir fait trois fois le tour du globe.

If I go on the ocean I shall charm all the fish and the fishermen will curse me for the fish will be a hundred years old thanks to having been around the globe three times.

(Le Grand Jeu I, 121)

The more one is inclined to read passages patterned after this one from the point of view of reason, the more one is likely to be persuaded that the essential characteristics of Péret's verse are arbitrariness, inconsequence, and impertinence. This is because the conjunction actually dislocates the reasonable sequence we are accustomed to see it sustain. In the following lines, for example, after beginning with a simple statement modeled after the silly exercises we associate with teach-yourself language textbooks, Péret proceeds to a justificatory clause that requires his readers to move further away from what common sense tells us is acceptable. Then he makes a final affirmation that sums up his lack of concern to effect a reconciliation with reason:

Les canards des astres ne sont pas ceux de ma soeur
car ma soeur est noire comme une huître
et de sa voix sortent des taupes
et les taupes de ma soeur gardent leur secret

The stars' ducks are not my sister's
for my sister is black as an oyster
and from her voice emerge moles
and my sister's moles keep their secret[5]

(Dormir, dormir dans les pierres [1926] I, 48–49)

Typically "for" serves primarily to open up reality in Péret's poetry, in a manner that gives weight to the definition of a poet, in *Le Déshonneur des poètes*, as "an inventor for whom discovery is but a means for attaining a new discovery":

> car une source coule de mon genou
> emportant ma hache vers d'autres continents
>
> for a spring flows from my knee
> carrying my axe toward other continents
> (*Le Grand Jeu* I, 226)

Under the conditions universally obtaining in Péret's verse, one may feel tempted to give special stress to the confession he makes in a poem from *Immortelle Maladie*: "car c'est l'inverse que je vois" ("for it is the opposite that I see" [I, 64]). In fact, though, one would do better to bear in mind that Benjamin Péret never ceased to see the scale of values we perceive consciously as "the rational product of absurd and horrible social constraints," castigated in his essay "La Pensée est UNE et indivisible."

To accuse Péret of undermining reality is to miss something fundamental, which cannot be ignored so long as we remember that "conscious reality" represented in his eyes a deformation of reality by rationalist education. From where Péret stood, the things evoked in his verse were, no less than in his stories, a rectification of reality, resulting from a process having the effect of eliminating the adverse effects of the deforming prism of rationalist education, and so anticipating the time to which Péret looked forward in his *Anthologie des Mythes*, when "poetic thought will have become once again as natural to man as seeing and sleeping" (29).

IV *And of course "but"*

An understanding of the line of thinking that was natural to Benjamin Péret facilitates comprehending that, where "because" and "for" affirm a liberty that common sense is powerless to resist, the conjunction "but" raises no objection to their revelations. On the contrary, in Péret's verse its role is to second the other two in their revolt against the limitations of reason. Although "but" serves, as might be expected, to qualify a preceding statement, as it does in customary usage, it never has the effect in Péret's writings of reducing the distance between that statement and rational conjecture. Péret used "but" as though his aim were to attain higher levels of irrational conjecture. A succession of far-fetched injunctions in one of his poems culminates in this qualification:

mais ne jamais insulter le facteur pour chasser les souris de la pendule qui attaqueraient les bronzes d'art à coups de bec

but never insult the mailman to frighten off the clock's mice
which would attack the artistic bronzes by pecking them
(*À Tâtons* [1947] II, 203)

Just as "but" qualifies without confining imaginative freedom, so when used to propose alternatives it helps conduct us further still into the world of imagination, instead of leading us back into the everyday world. Thus one poem takes us

au delà de la grande plaine glacière où les dinosaures couvent encore leurs œufs d'où ne sortiront pas de tulipes d'hématites mais des caravanes de hérissons au ventre bleu

beyond the great glacial plain where the dinosaurs still sit on
their eggs from which will emerge not hematite tulips
but caravans of blue-bellied hedgehogs
(*Je sublime* [1936] II, 126)

V   *Intuition and Desire*

One could multiply examples, adding for good measure instances of how Péret used "of," "in order that," "however," and so on, which contribute to his poems in the same way as the conjunctions considered above. But sufficient evidence is available already to allow us to sketch a few conclusions.

Whenever Péret's conjunctions are viewed in context, two factors can be observed governing their use. One of these is the influence exerted by a mode of intuition to which we have heard him allude frequently. The other, about which we have had considerably less forewarning, is desire.

Benjamin Péret's major contribution to Surrealism is, possibly, to have made intuition and desire, as he speaks of them, interdependent elements in poetic expression. True enough, in his published comments on the nature and function of poetry, he characteristically refrained from emphatically relating desire to intuition. Only indirectly did he consent to share his opinions with his public, displaying typical discretion in two comparatively long prefaces, the first to his *Anthologie des Mythes, légendes et contes populaires d'Amérique*, the second introducing his 1956 *Anthologie de l'Amour sublime*.

We know from the essay "La Pensée est UNE et indivisible" that Péret regarded poetic intuition as supremely important, acknowledging the fundamental fact that, in a society ruled by reason and reluctant to admit that poetry is destined to "reveal the future of the world," intuition of the sort which preoccupied him as a poet must encounter antagonism, especially when taking its most audacious form, that of prophetic intuition, operating beyond the bounds of reasonable projection. Still, there is a danger we may misconstrue the true nature of Péret's poetic effort, if our understanding of its orientation is limited to identifying in his poems evidence of persistent opposition to rationality. Beyond question, use of automatism aided Péret in freeing himself from the constraints of reason. But had his purpose been to achieve this end only, then automatism would have been for him simply a technique (and perhaps not the most efficient one available) employed to bring about certain foreseeable results. Although the discoveries Péret made through automatic writing tend, initially, to attract or repel readers thanks to their irrational quality, full appreciation of his poetry calls for something more than the ability to see where this or that poem goes beyond rational limits. To progress further with Péret, we have to consider that he looked upon thought as indivisible because he saw no valid distinction between reason and unreason. The weakness of rationality, therefore, seemed to Benjamin Péret to lie in its incapacity to acknowledge the essential unity of prelogical thought (poetry) and the logical thought supporting rational discourse.

Knowing already that *L'Anthologie des Mythes* refers to a significant connection between poetic intuition and the unconscious, we have only to recall that in "La Pensée est UNE et indivisible" Péret speaks of desire as resident in the unconscious, in order to grasp that desire and intuition were interconnected, in his mind. But where does this take us? *Le Déshonneur des poètes* facilitates answering this question by revealing that Péret, who equated poetry with intuition, saw it also as love (72). This is why, evidently, he felt entitled to speak in his *Anthologie de l'Amour sublime* of the nineteenth century in France as the period that liberated sensibility by "pleading in favor of the marvelous and of love, which amounts to proposing an irrationality, denied and mocked up until then" (10). This implication of a close relationship between love and the marvelous in the realm of the irrational is important, since it allowed Péret to lay the foundation of a myth of "sublime love," originating in desire.

One may still wonder what is to be gained by following Péret into a discussion of love, when we are still dealing with his use of conjunctions. The advantage of doing so comes to our notice when we see him emphasize that, in sublime love, the marvelous loses the "extraterrestrial supernatural character" with which earlier myths invested it. In sublime love, runs Péret's argument, the marvelous "returns so to speak to its source to discover its true outlet and to take its place within the limits of human existence" (20).

Beneath the surface of Péret's discussion of love and desire lies a conception of poetry that is never quite given explicit development, but to which his poems nevertheless make us sensitive. Here we become responsive to an undercurrent of meaning which, in its turn, helps illuminate his verse, as, for example, we listen to Péret declare that sublime love takes its origin in primordial aspirations, so effecting a transmutation that produces an agreement between body and spirit "tending to melt them into a higher unity in which the one can no longer be distinguished from the other." We become especially responsive to his meaning when he goes on to assert, "Desire finds itself charged with bringing about this fusion that is its ultimate justification" (20). Of course, it is not possible to interpret every phrase used by Péret on this occasion as though it applied to the act of poetic creation. All the same, the role of grammatical structure in fusing elements rearranged at the bidding of nonrational intuition interestingly parallels that of desire, as we find references to its effects in the *Anthologie de l'Amour sublime*. Specifically, the way Péret uses conjunctions makes us witness in his poems the operation of desire as it is presented in the *Anthologie des Myths*: "multiplied by its own satisfaction" (25). And so we appreciate more readily "the complete abandon" without which, we are assured in the *Anthologie de l'Amour sublime*, "no true love is conceivable" (8).

Presenting his anthology of sublime love, Péret asked pertinently whether it is only the poet who can experience love in its sublime form. Replying affirmatively to his own question, he insisted nonetheless that the poet is not a writer of poems so much as someone capable of detecting the presence of poetry: "He is not a stranger to poetry who, even placed on ground level, discovers in everything its heavenly aspect" (70). Given Benjamin Péret's contempt for religious solutions to human problems, this reference to the heavenly aspect of things is quite unambiguous. In his *Anthologie de l'Amour sublime* it marks his profound opposition to the incomplete sense of reality which reason is forever limited to encompassing. When he speaks of detecting the presence of poetry, of "recognizing poetry," he really means glimpsing that enlarged sense of reality called Surreality. In other words, he is talking of being responsive to the dictates of desire, for which sublime love is but one mode of expression. Thus, if we probe the deeper implications of desire, we go with Péret beyond emotional involvement, however passionately communicated. We understand better where he is leading us now, when we read his declaration to the effect that desire undertakes to fill the void inherent in human life with another human being—someone with whom it is possible to form "an harmonious whole." Granted divinity by desire, a person of the opposite sex at the same time confers divinity. Hence "this double operation, by its irrational character, participates in the marvelous" (61).

We shall have occasion to return to this operation, as it is reflected in Péret's love poems. For the present, Péret's description of it is of assistance to us in giving due emphasis to his use of conjunctions in the face of reason's protest. Conjunctions externalize the nonrational, which, in Péret's estimation, leads directly to poetry. They undermine the barricade separating the rational from the irrational. Or, to borrow a figure the poet himself has used, they fill the void inherent in the human condition, as they reduce the distance between physical reality and the realm of desire.

Péret's use of conjunctions testifies to that "reaching out" toward the complete happiness which man expects when he ceases, as the *Anthologie de l'Amour sublime* predicts, to feel torn apart (21). This is why they bring to our attention that "double automatic movement, centrifugal and centripetal," mentioned in the *Anthologie des Mythes*, by which desire finds fulfillment in his verse. In this sense, the function of conjunctions is to highlight desire, which the *Anthologie de l'Amour sublime* likens to a mariner's compass (75). If we neglect to keep that compass in sight, we soon lose our way in Péret's poetic universe. But if we are able to remain attentive to its movements, unpredictable though common sense may find them, then we enjoy the benefits of the kind of magic that the *Anthologie des Mythes* calls "the flesh and blood of poetry" (23).

VI *A Generalized Principle of Mutation*

Considered in this perspective, the effect of a principle which, because it runs counter to our preconceptions about the proper role of conjunctions in linguistic exchange, appeared earlier to merit the adjective "disjunctive," can now be seen in a significantly different light.

Referring to the efforts that have been made from time to time to draw poetry and art into the field of science, Péret once remarked, "The enterprise has always failed and will fail again, because poetry and art live fully in intuition, by and for intuition, and their means of action is imagination."[6] Science, on the other hand, appeared to him to rest upon experimentation and to proceed by logical deduction. The two forms of cognition, intuition and science, were one, in his view, only when human thought was "undifferentiated"—"just as all higher forms of life come together in the egg." Since that time, he contended, they have moved further and further apart so that intuition remains "the fertilizing element of all thought, even scientific thought," while science "has added nothing to poetry and art." Hence it is intuition that continues to be "the seeing-eye dog" for reason, not vice versa.

Viewed from the vantage point of this statement, Péret's conjunctions, at variance with accepted usage, challenge us to forsake the habits of deductive thought from which usage draws strength. In this, their function is neither to bring about willful destruction nor to promote incoherence. Rather, they facilitate that rectification of our sense of reality to which, in Péret's estimation, poets worthy of the name are dedicated. Which came first, the chicken or the egg? Péret's answer to the old question, as formulated in "La Soupe déshydratée," is that "the egg is at once egg, cock, and hen" (51). The idea of poetry as self-generative and therefore self-sufficient finds assured expression here, interestingly opening up another question—that of the value of abstract art. "Abstract art," Péret declared in the same context, "makes us witness an entirely different, indeed contrary, process: the cock is metamorphosed into a hard-boiled egg that can be peeled and eaten if one feels the desire, but the evolution stops there, unless one wishes to include the phenomena of digestion entailed by the absorption of the hard-boiled egg."

A characteristic result of the use of conjunctions in Péret's verse is that it often endows imaginative inventiveness with the kind of increased momentum that seemed to him lacking in abstract art. Conjunctions do not merely confirm that Benjamin Péret was held back by no nostalgia for the everyday world, left behind as he advanced into the marvelous. They testify also to the magnetism of intuitive forces, scientifically indefinable, urging him to go farther into the unusual. Hence the movement with which conjunctions invest his poems is in marked contrast with the stasis of everyday existence. They promote unrestrained transformations, unfettered progress from one phase of experience, one mode of perception, to another.

If Peret's use of conjunctions were to be considered simply as evidence of a technique, deliberately adopted and purposefully employed, it would be far less interesting than it actually is. Conjunctions would not be worthy of special attention in his poems, if they did not come to play a role that, evaluated from the theoretical position he adopted and defended, can be qualified as truly poetic. Since these are poetic elements that find release naturally in the process of automatic writing, they never offer any hint of imaginative strain or self-conscious striving for effect. On the contrary, they lend themselves everywhere to the welcome enrichment of effects brought to the surface of consciousness by the automatic method, prolonging these in the direction to which Benjamin Péret's imagination persistently inclined, so playing their essential part in precipitating the marvelous.

CHAPTER 6

Mechanics of the Marvelous
II: Prepositions

I Plunging Into the Unknown

IF such a thing as a rattlesnake exists, then why could there
not be a spectacled snake? Benjamin Péret does not ask this
question in so many words. Instead, he leaves it with us, in the
poem "Nuits blanches" (Sleepless Nights), from his *De Derrière
les fagots* (1934), when he refers to both a *serpent à sonnettes*
and a *serpent à lunettes*. In doing so, he brings to mind two
texts, both published a short time before *De Derrière les fagots*.

In the first, André Breton's *Second Manifeste du surréalisme*,
printed in the last number of *La Révolution surréaliste* in 1929,
before separate publication in 1930, we come upon a reference
to the crucial problem that Surrealism undertook to raise, from
the twenties onward: *"that of human expression in all its forms."*
It is here that Breton continues with the comment "Whoever
says expression says, to begin with, language. You must not
be surprised, then, to see surrealism situated first of all almost
exclusively on the plane of language..." (183). The immediate
advantage the first Surrealists felt to lie with language is that
its use is subject, theoretically, to none of the coercive pressures
that weigh, for instance, upon social and political activity.
Nothing, in principle, denies us the privilege of thinking about
spectacled snakes. As Breton asks pertinently in his *Introduction
au discours sur le peu de réalité* (1927), "Does not the medi-
ocrity of our universe depend upon our power of enunciation?"
All the same, it is a long step from talking about a snake found
in the animal kingdom to speaking of one, like Péret's spectacled
reptile, that exists nowhere in the world. How are we to succeed
in taking such a step, supposing we are inclined to do so?

89

This question sends us back to the second text deserving of mention in connection with Péret's allusion to a *serpent à lunettes*: Raymond Roussel's *Comment j'ai écrit certains de mes livres* (How I Wrote Certain of my Books), published in 1935. As an explanatory public statement by an enigmatic independent writer whom the Surrealists held in the highest esteem, Roussel's essay is of considerable interest. Its special significance for our purposes is that it supplies details about Roussel's method of composition that will enable us to adopt the correct perspective for evaluating Péret's use of prepositions.

"I would choose a word," declares Roussel, "then join it to another with the preposition *à*; and these two words, understood in a sense different from the original, furnished me with a new creation. . . . I must say that this initial work was difficult and already took a lot of my time."[1] The more he prolongs this explanation, the clearer Roussel makes it that his method was a most deliberate one. First finding a word that lent itself to two interpretations, he then tried, so he tells us, to "marry" the first word to a second that also could be understood in two ways and that lent itself to connection with the first by means of the preposition selected—"and this was, I repeat, a lot of time-consuming work." What took time, evidently, was the calculation of effects. The element of deliberate choice was paramount, so that whenever surprise results followed, these can be assumed to have been meticulously engineered. With every justification, Roussel could speak proudly of his technique as a "procédé très spécial" (11).[2] Whatever else it accomplished, it set his writings at the opposite pole from Péret's.

Benjamin Péret sought to improve his power of enunciation by no *procédé*, no procedure or method to which he resorted consciously. In this, he stood as far apart from Roussel (who found the application of a method not merely fruitful but necessary) as from the painter Max Ernst, who, during his period of association with Surrealism, took advantage of the mechanical process of *frottage* as, he tells us, "a means of forcing inspiration."[3] Specifically, Benjamin Péret's way of using prepositions points to a different conception of poetry from the one that led Raymond Roussel to assert, with respect to the "unforeseen creations due to phonic combinations" characteristic of his own work, "It is essentially a poetic process" (23). For Péret, poetry and process were incompatible, unless we are to understand verbal automatism as a process. In Péret's automatic texts, prepositions link words according to no preestablished formula that the poet finds benefit in applying.

None of this authorizes our setting Péret above Roussel. The important thing is that the operation of imaginative invention in Péret was diametrically opposed to the technique Roussel took pride in offering for possible development by writers coming after him. We begin to become aware of the distance separating these two authors when we consider how the preposition the latter liked to employ functions in the work of the former.

As it is used by Benjamin Péret, *à* lends itself to a variety of purposes that may be classified for convenience under two headings, according to whether it denotes association ("with") or purpose ("for"). In Péret's writings, of course, these categories are at best provisional and likely to appear arbitrary at times—notably where *à* seems to link words unconventionally, in defiance of habitual thought and familiar situations. In spite of their weaknesses, however, such categories serve to mark the range of effects that can result when imagination unrestrained avails itself freely of prepositions, so as to indicate relationships between words that, within the context of Péret's poetry, do not depend upon reasonable preconception for authority, that is, for the right to our attention.

So far as we can speak of one of our categories as grouping easier examples for examination than the other, it is surely the first, which merely confronts us with the linkage of two substantives by an apparently innocuous preposition. On a single page, the second poem of *Dormir, dormir dans les pierres* offers several instances of this prepositional function: *"des liquides aux oreilles de soupçon"* ("liquids with ears of suspicion"), *"l'orage aux yeux de paon"* ("the peacock-eyed storm"), *"les gares aux gestes de miroir"* ("the railroad stations with mirror gestures"), *"les grands hérons aux lèvres de sel éternels et cruels"* ("the great salt-lipped herons eternal and cruel"). It is evident that, as is the case with Péret's handling of conjunctions, this use of the preposition is simple on the level of verbal structure only. When examined from the standpoint of reasonable association, of everyday experience, of precedent, the linkage of two nouns in such a manner is far from a simple matter.

What Péret accomplishes may appear perplexing. When this happens, it is the function of *à* to make us see sights unprecedented in the world with which we are acquainted. *De Derrière les fagots,* for example, shows us bearded soap (II, 101), an egg on wheels (II, 106), and a handkerchief with stained-glass windows (II, 29). *Le Grand Jeu's* contribution is the sight of insects with carapaces of glass (I, 159). *Trois Cerises et une sardine* (1936) has spectators whose heads are made of fence, covered with nasturtiums (II, 147), as well as a fresh lance with the brains of a lettuce (II, 173). In *A Tâtons* a wave in the rising tide wears blinders (II, 206).

As we look back from the point we have now reached, considering the result obtained in relation to Péret's conception of poetry as a confrontation with the marvelous, what impresses most is that he was able to achieve so much by such uncomplex means. This is especially noteworthy when we observe something that occurs in a number of instances. Linking words in unprecedented ways has the consequence of throwing the reader into uncertainty about the significance to be attached to nouns now brought into unwonted proximity. Is the fence that serves as a head for the spectators mentioned in *Trois Cerises et une sardine* made of nasturtiums, as noted above, or of capuchine nuns? Who can tell, when the word *capucines* has both senses in French? And does the big wave of which we hear in *A Tâtons* ("*une grande vague à œillères*" [II, 206]) have blinders or eyeteeth? Anyone who objects to ambiguity of this kind will find little to satisfy him in Eluard's grand declaration, in his 1929 essay on Péret: "Imagination does not have an instinct for imitation."

Since the phenomena brought together by the prepositional *à* in Péret's verse have been released from the world of common experience, we must expect their definition to resist, from time to time at any rate, the limitations that would arise in a rationally viable situation. Under normal circumstances, the reasoning mind's inclination to address itself immediately to the most reasonable interpretation would meet with no resistance. But under the circumstances prevailing in Péret's poetic universe, reason finds itself denied the benefits it usually derives from observation of a rational sequence of ideas or events. When eggs have nothing in common, reasonably speaking, with aigrettes, it is impossible for common sense to know whether, in one phrase from *Le Grand Jeu* (I, 117), *les œufs aux aigrettes de soie*, "aigrettes" takes its force from the vocabulary of ornithology, electricity, or costumery—especially when it is qualified by the adjective "silky." The difficulty is the same when we read *les ressorts à boudins* in *Dernier Malheur, dernièr chance* (1956 [II, 109]): is Péret linking springs with blood puddings, fat pudgy fingers, or corkscrew curls? The fact is, of course, that he is doing all this at once. Meanings proliferate, spinning off from a center of attention, established by the word preceding *à*, in a variety of directions opened up to the reader's imagination by the word following. André Breton once spoke of everything that exists objectively as standing at the center of an ever-widening circle of possibilities, and he went on to define the imaginary as "that which tends to become real." As for Benjamin Péret, he brought to this statement the authority of practical illustration.

The use of *à* to denote purpose, in which the preposition appears to have a more sophisticated role, produces comparable results: the storm race (*"la course à l'orage"*) in *Le Grand Jeu* (I, 150) and the light box (*"la boîte aux lumières"* [I, 192]), analogous to the letter box (*la boîte aux lettres*). More interesting, though, is that *à*, employed this way, sometimes confronts us with a complex situation, even more challenging to our preconceptions, when it makes possible the linkage of noun and verb.

Here and there, it is true, the noun–verb combination produces no effect that we have not seen generated by the combination of noun with noun. In *Le Grand Jeu* we read of a road eel for rolling in the stomach (*"Anguille de route à rouler dans l'estomac"* [I, 121]). In like fashion, *Dernier Malheur, dernière chance* speaks of water to be cut into slices (*"une eau à découper en tranches"* [II, 169]). In more striking conflict with reasonable expectation, however, are those instances where the sense of *à* is expanded, so that now its force can no longer be rendered simply by "for." *Dernier Malheur, dernière chance* brings to our notice, among other things, *"un talon / pressé de murmurer des mots à liquifier le marbre qui l'écoute"*: a heel in a hurry to murmur words suitable for [capable of] liquifying the marble that is listening to it (II, 169). This use of *à* is rare in Péret's verse, but not unique:

> Et le verre blanc des bouteilles n'acceptait
>   plus que le contact du vin rouge
> à cause de la fièvre jaune qui soufflait dans
>   ses doigts
> un air à faire se dresser les cheveux de pierre
> des navires en perdition à l'entrée d'un port

> And the bottles' white glass no longer accepted
>   any contact but that of red wine
> because of the yellow fever blowing on
>   its fingers
> a tune suitable for [capable of] making the
>   stone hair stand on end
> on the ships in distress at the entrance to a port
> *(De Derrière les fagots* [II, 36])

The ambiguity that results from coupling suitability with capability impresses itself upon us because, by introducing a verb, *à* highlights an activity that implicates the noun preceding it and the one depending on the verb following. For this reason, examples such as the ones cited may be said to merit discussion most appropriately in connection with Péret's use of verbs that liberate the marvelous. For the time being, it will suffice to notice how *à* makes possible the fusion of substantive to verb in a way that generates an activity totally consistent with the antirational impression that this same preposition summons up when it joins two nouns: everywhere it helps Péret achieve his ambition as a poet—to plunge into the unknown.

II *Poetry Seeks to Find Expression*

The preposition *de* occurs more frequently in Péret's work than does *à*. It is as if he finds it more suitable to the depiction of the universe that his verse explores; first in its sense of "belonging to," in its possessive function; and secondly with the force that "of" has in English and, more particularly, "made of."

Taken in its first sense, *de* allows Péret to refer in *De Derrière les fagots* to the temptation of closed umbrellas (*"la tentation des parapluies fermés"* [II, 25]) and to moles' points of suspension (*"les points de suspension des taupes"*), over which, incidentally, flying mushrooms describe perfect parabolas (II, 31). In *Le Grand Jeu*, it is the vagina's rainbow (*"l'arc-en-ciel du vagin"*) that catches his attention (I, 174). However, despite the potential for disconcerting ambiguity to be detected when *de* is used in this way (do closed umbrellas exert temptation or experience it?), it is not in its possessive sense that *de* is called upon to make its most noteworthy contribution to Péret's poems.

At first, where *de* means "of" its role is to interconnect two previously unrelated elements. In *Le Grand Jeu* it offers us a deep-sea diver of fire (I, 162), centuries of coal, and lanterns of dry glue (I, 196). From *De Derrière les fagots* come seedbeds of Grecian noses and the strident cry of red eggs, as well as steaks' tears (II, 32).

The direction in which Péret's imagination leads him becomes more clearly visible as we notice that his poems align words in a way that violates all our preconceptions about which elements appropriately may serve to make up the objects we have the opportunity to see represented. Word groupings repeatedly derail rational thought, as they demonstrate that Péret's poetic universe is a world peopled not by ethereal abstractions but by hauntingly concrete presences. His two longest collections, *De Derrière les fagots* and *Le Grand Jeu*, both repeatedly illustrate the contribution that *de* can make in this connection. From the former come birds of flour (II, 39), magnificent mink-coat ships called dandelion flowers (II, 48), greenwood hats, white-wine shoes, and months of soap (II, 57), a butter violin (II, 75), long white hands with nails of fresh greenery (II, 86), and water-lilies of suspenders (II, 105). Turning to *Le Grand Jeu*, we find a strange character with eyes of bark and bitter almonds (I, 164), a pretty dancer, naked under a salt coat (I, 73), wool oranges (I, 200), and another young woman who wraps herself in a coat of feet, said to be as light as a summer hat (I, 108).

All this is consonant with the role we have already seen assumed by a general principle of mutation, operating in Péret's work in a way that breaks down the classifications people customarily think of as ordering physical reality. The same may be said of the contribution made by the preposition *en*. This is only to be expected, when *en* carries a meaning not far removed from that of *de*: "in the shape of." Thus heads, in *Le Grand Jeu*, rest on legs in the shape of 1919 (I, 122), and in *De Derrière les fagots* are pretty microbes in the form of barometers (II, 33), trumpet-shaped noses that play a funeral march (II, 60), and malefactors in the shape of tunnels (II, 95).

Where *en* means "made of," it takes us even farther along the road that Péret's poems invite us to travel. *De Derrière les fagots* shows us pince-nez made of coal and at the same time of pumice stone, or perhaps stencil ink (II, 46). A poem Péret wrote the summer before he died, "Dans le Vent" (In the Wind), has a house made of watch springs in continuous movement, with a door of terror-stricken doe's eyes (II, 299). In addition, it shows us a room furnished with a table made of the harrowing cries of an osprey and chairs of wolves' jaws ready to swallow everything up.

III   *Resisting General Domestication*

With Raymond Roussel, writing was always a matter of attempting to reconcile, imaginatively, two elements that had nothing in common. The words he linked by *à*, for instance, provided, in their primary sense, the point of departure for a narrative development designed to culminate in some kind of justification for understanding the same words in their alternative sense. Yet, however Roussel played with words, he always looked to imagination to earn approval for the game in which he was engaged. Thus for him imagination had a prescribed role, to be filled within definite limits—arranging narrative events, for example, so as to connect his first phrase constructed by means of *à* to the second. Benjamin Péret, in sharp contrast, had no conscious motives that would make possible a comparison between his use of imagination and Roussel's. Bringing words together into unforeseen relationships by means of prepositions, Péret achieved results that were markedly different from those to which Roussel habitually attached importance.

In Péret's work, prepositions facilitate communication between disparate and apparently mutually exclusive phenomena; thus attacking the idea of physical reality as appropriately categorized. The familiar world no longer exercises censorship over imaginative play. It is divested of the right of arbitration, so far as the consequences of prepositional linkage are concerned. Instead, imagination is permitted to take from the physical universe only what it needs, free to utilize whatever it borrows in disregard of the reality principle. And so, with Péret, we are reminded once again that another Surrealist, André Breton, once declared that imagination does not have to "humiliate itself before life," because the imaginary "is that which tends to become real."[4]

As it functions in Péret's writing, the preposition underscores the poet's gift for making connections between elements that reason insists ought to be kept apart, and for identifying relationships where common sense acknowledges none. Therefore one fundamental question is clear. It has been amusingly formulated by Lewis Carroll:

"When *I* use a word," Humpty Dumpty said, in a rather scornful tone, "it means just what I choose it to mean—neither more nor less."

"The question is," said Alice, "whether you *can* make words mean so many different things."

"The question is," said Humpty Dumpty, "which is to be the master—that's all."

There can be no doubt about how Péret would reply, since his work demonstrates his agreement with the first Surrealist manifesto, which defined automatic expression as "the dictation of thought in the absence of all control exercised by reason, outside all aesthetic or moral preoccupations" (40). Once automatism had begun to release in him the marvels that rational thought "disperses,"[5] Péret's poetic sensibility was at liberty to bring together the supposedly irreconcilable and to establish equivalences which require that our apperception of what is real change radically. In other words, Péret's attack on the utilitarian, undertaken in the name of Surrealism, was carried out under impetus from the pleasure principle.

Citing a phrase by Charles Etienne to the effect that language always serves to express something, Benjamin Péret added in his article "La Soupe déshydratée," "I would specify only that this something pre-exists the language that has the ambition to express it" (52). Much of the trouble the reasonable mind experiences, when confronted with Péret's verse, has but one source. The strange things that prepositions help bring to the level of linguistic expression exist here in defiance of rational projection and of literary tradition. The latter admits symbolic formulation and does not protest when its meaning is hard to penetrate—but only so long as symbolic intent does not elude interpretation altogether. Péret's imaginative creations are not symbolic, though. They stand in their own right, aggressive representations of the poetic principle which, as Péret applied it, is an outlaw principle. This is something Pierre Naville—who coedited *La Révolution surréaliste* with him—was not slow to grasp: "This wave that serves as his life," wrote Naville, "this imagination which for him takes the place of reason, can never be granted the aim of poetic symbolism: they are poetry itself."[6]

As practiced by Benjamin Péret, poetry does not reside in language so much as in that to which language alludes. Language for him was what Surrealism meant it to be: the means of bringing the impossible within the bounds of the possible. On the theoretical level, the role of poetry as he saw it might pass unchallenged. It was only with its practical application that he drew criticism.

To the extent that we are all accustomed to encountering poetry through language, we incline to identify the former with the latter, especially in the measure that we share a tendency to question the poet's right to use language in order to refer to something that familiar reality and generally recognized human emotions and behavior patterns do not certify as authentic. In consequence, Benjamin Péret enjoys a limited popularity. And he pays this price because, of all the Surrealists, he was the one who applied the celebrated dictum from the *Manifesto of Surrealism* with the greatest rigor: "Language has been given man so that he may make surrealist use of it." The Surrealist use of language meant, in Péret's case, exceeding by far the limits for poetic license indulgently, but watchfully, set by society.

It was presumably to the trend that characterizes Surrealist writing, and which Péret's work exemplifies as does no other, that Ferdinand Alquié was referring, when he spoke of Surrealism as creating "objectively noninterpretable poetry" and attributed to Benjamin Péret an essential role in effecting a form of "purification" that "brought to light the very essence of all poetry."[7]

Alquié went on to refer to Péret's imagery as "evident and devoid of logical sense," speaking of his "images discouraging all explication in rational or textbook style." The example chosen to illustrate this contention is familiar to us: "the strident cry of red eggs." This is the one that Paul Eluard had selected, in his *prière d'insérer* for *De Derrière les fagots,* from which the phrase comes. It is clear that Alquié leaned heavily on Eluard's argument, from which he borrowed the adjective "evident."[8] Where Alquié comments, "Here, the absurd becomes irrefutable truth," Eluard probes deeper:

One of the principal properties of poetry is to inspire in frauds a grimace that unmasks them and lets them be judged. Like no other, the poetry of Benjamin Péret encourages this reaction, as inevitable as it is useful. For it is endowed with that major accent, eternal and modern, which detonates and makes a hole in a world of prudently ordered necessities and of babbling old refrains. For it tends with its extralucid images, its images as clear as rock-water, evident like *the strident cry of red eggs,* toward a perfect comprehension of the unwonted and toward its use against the ravages of malignant exploitation by stupidity and a certain form of good sense. For it militates insolently in favor of a new *regime,* that of logic linked with life not like a shadow but like a star.[9]

This estimate of the essential qualities of Péret's writing is especially noteworthy, coming from a fellow Surrealist whose verse could never compete with Péret's "specifically subversive poetry that has the color of the future." The key to Eluard's admiration for Péret, evidently, is to be found in the subversive nature of the latter's poems. It was certainly his gift for subversion that guaranteed Péret a privileged place among those whom André Breton called friends. Fifteen years after *De Derrière les fagots* appeared, Breton was insisting:

For my part, I honor more than ever today, because they are so rare, works electrified by the need for subversion that alone is capable of showing the capacity of individual resistance opposed to general domestication. On condition of course that the means placed at the disposal of subversion are up to its level, poverty of means being of a nature to compromise it radically. In the face of present-day strangulation of "revolutionary" ideas by those very people who claim for themselves the monopoly on these ideas, the subjection of these ideas to a rule that cannot be broken and that stays their growth, the historical chances that these ideas will be corrupted and the certainty of seeing them put forward by people who share them not at all but, in the strange period we live in, find real material advantage in them, subversion, as it is practiced in art in particular, remains the great reservoir of new strength; it alone today can claim to assume to the fullest extent human protest against absurdity, inertia and flagrant injustice in every form.[10]

Breton's statement is doubly valuable. First, it makes us aware of the reasons for which, as a Surrealist, Benjamin Péret never confused revolutionary activism with the writing of texts directly inspired by his sociopolitical views, even though he agreed wholeheartedly with what Breton wrote in his *Légitime Défense* (1926): "It seems to us that revolt alone is creative." Second, it expands upon the remark made by Breton about Péret, in his *Anthologie de l'Humour noir.* Here we read notably that Péret disposed of "the crust of exclusive signification with which usage has covered all words and which leaves practically no play in associations between them, outside the pigeonholes to which they are confined in little groups by immediate or agreed use, solidly supported by routine" (505). The revolutionary role granted prepositions, in Péret's poems, is therefore to assist in destroying the "narrow compartment that opposes any new relationship between signifying elements which today are frozen into words" and so "ceaselessly increases the zone of opacity that alienates man from nature and from himself."[11] As they play the part reserved for them, prepositions remind us that, according to the first Surrealist manifesto, "resting upon the belief in the superior reality of certain forms of association" (40), Surrealism discards "all other psychic mechanisms when setting out to resolve the principal problems of life." Hence, remarks Breton in his *Les Vases communicants* (1932), "To compare two subjects as distant as possible from one another, or, by any other method, to bring them suddenly and strikingly face to face, remains the highest task to which poetry can aspire."[12]

Whereas Raymond Roussel spoke in *Comment j'ai écrit certains de mes livres* of a "problem," which he undertook to resolve imaginatively, Benjamin Péret, seeing no problem that need detain him, placed his trust in an imaginative interpretation of reality that, through automatic writing, would leave its poetic imprint on language. As prepositions assume their role in his verse collections, they offer evidence of the utmost importance for a comprehension of the meaning that Péret attached to poetry.

There is in Surrealism a deep and abiding respect for words, as automatism permits them to surface in consciousness. Reluctance to engage in revision or to carry out editorial changes is not a sign of bravado but proof of the Surrealist's confidence in the poetic richness of uninhibited verbal flow. And no one has ever demonstrated greater fidelity to the tenets of Surrealism, as summarized here, than did Benjamin Péret. Rather than respecting the barriers that, in everyday reasonable exchange, separate some words from others, prepositions in his writings serve to make words freely available to the imagination. They demonstrate that, in poetic expression, such barriers must be cast down. This is why prepositions establish an essential link between the language that society has taught us and attainment of a liberty that society hedges about with restrictions and constraints to which rationality lends an air of permanence.

Had Péret employed prepositions as a technical device, intended to contribute to the elaboration of an original viewpoint upon reality, yet upon a world still recognizable as the one we all knew before we came to his poems, then his poetic practice would have run counter to his theory, which depicts the poet as a revolutionary advancing at the head of mankind. As prepositions play their part in his poems, they make it possible for us to see the following. To Péret, the revolutionary poet could never be a versifier, treating his writings as the vehicle for inflammatory political or social ideas. No, the effect produced by Péret's prepositions points to revolution advocated and experienced at a deeper level, at the level of sensibility itself. Consideration of the poetic role of verbs in the poetry of Benjamin Péret helps show better what this means.

CHAPTER 7

Mechanics of the Marvelous
III: Verbs

I "The Triumphant Cry of the Ruby Bursting From Its Matrix"[1]

IT seems that beginning a discussion of verbs, as Benjamin Péret employed them, with the remark that we cannot ignore their presence in his writing is to start with a statement so banal as to be devoid of value. Yet verbs claim our attention in his work so dramatically that something obviously true of every writer assumes special force when we are speaking of Péret. The very first poem of his first published collection, *Le Passager du transatlantique*, accords verbs a role which everything that followed shows to be characteristic:

> En avant disait l'arc-en-ciel matinal
> En avant pour les soupiraux de notre jeunesse
> Nous avons éclaté
> et tout ce qui était bleu est resté bleu

> Forward the morning rainbow was saying
> Forward to the ventilators of our youth
> We've burst
> and all that was blue has remained blue

(I, 15)

Familiarity with Péret's poems will confirm that they give verbs prominence not simply because every sentence needs a verb but because of the special direction verbal structures impose upon his writing: a rainbow unaccountably endowed with the power of speech first talks of something rationally inexplicable—the ventilators of our youth—and then uses a verb

103

(*éclater*) that denotes either violent activity or a process of
germination—both recurrent features of Péret's writing.

Two verbs in particular point to the attraction of the theme
of germination for Péret's imagination: *fleurir* ("to blossom")
and *jaillir* ("to burst forth"). For what it will lead us to expect
of his poems, the significant thing to notice is that in most cases
Péret's use of these verbs denotes abrupt departure from familiar
usage. They mark a striking transposition that can show us salads
suddenly blossoming on the top of crumbling triumphal arches
(II, 47), make us see eternal things blossom "like the cigarettes
I smoke out of nostalgia for atlases when I was ten" (I, 119),
and soap orchids about to blossom like a lamp humming Negro
songs (II, 239). Liquids in revolt burst forth "as bayonets thrust
themselves into the transparent chests of men" (I, 183) and
springs of old hair burst from paving stones (II, 43).

As for the theme of violence, sufficient on its own to prove
that Péret's is not a world of fairy-tale evasion, this is borne by
verbs referring to brutality, savagery, and inexplicable cruelty.
A poem from *De Derrière les fagots*, "Faire le pied de grue,"
opens:

> L'orage éclate au fond des plus secrets tiroirs
> et c'est la lutte à mort
> entre le peigne et le salsifis
>
> The storm breaks deep in the most secret drawers
> and now begins a struggle to the death
> between the comb and the oyster plant
>
> (II, 89)

In the same collection, various pins lie in wait in a fireplace
for a little glass lizard, "to beat it up" (II, 27). The poem
"Qui est-ce" begins:

> J'appelle tabac ce qui est oreille
> et les mites en profitent pour se jeter sur le jambon
> d'où un remarquable combat entre les sources
> jaillissant du pain d'épices
> et les lunettes qui empêchent les aveugles de voir clair

> I call tobacco that which is ear
> and moths take advantage of this to throw themselves
>   upon the ham
> there results a remarkable fight between the springs
> bursting from gingerbread
> and the spectacles that keep blind men from seeing
>   (II, 111)

The beginning of "Déjeté" is similar. Here sugar, wearing "a disgusting priest's cap," hurls itself upon a flower bed, trampling it in fury (II, 108).

Such violence is not peculiar to one phase of Péret's writing. In *Le Grand Jeu*, a violin, arriving in Toronto, breaks down a skyscraper full of hummingbirds (I, 187). A certain volcano mentioned in *Trois Cerises et une sardine* does not hesitate to massacre a few dozen grandmothers' breasts or railroad signals (II, 148). In one of Péret's last poems, "Nuit noire," written in August, 1959, big nettles "with satisfied banker's smiles," take pleasure in biting granite until it loses "its blood of fresh moss," uttering the sigh of a can of preserves being opened, and expiring "like a dandelion releasing its seeds" (II, 317).

From the outset, Péret's poetic language granted natural phenomena, as well as the curiously antinatural ones born of his imagination, autonomy of action, freedom of movement, the power of self-expression, and independence of thought by releasing them from the environment that familiarity has persuaded us to consider natural. To be sure, we encounter a certain number of poems in which, represented by the first-person authorial voice, man occupies the center of the stage. By and large, however, these are poems on the very personal theme of love, and as such they merit study on their own. More characteristically, Péret leaves phenomena borrowed from nature free to assert their presence for their own purposes and in their own way—by what they say, do, think, feel, desire. Thus a strange energy is generated everywhere in Péret's poems, finding an outlet through behavior for which there is no precedent in the world we know from daily experience. The reassurance most of us find in an anthropocentric interpretation of the world about us is undermined, and the consequences are far-reaching.

Considered from this angle, Péret's poems illustrate a theory formulated in his essay on the Surrealist painter Wifredo Lam: "The true mission of the artist—painter or poet—has always consisted in rediscovering within himself the archetypes underlying poetic thought, in bringing to bear upon these the weight of a new affectivity, in order that there shall circulate between himself and his fellow men an energetic current, all the more intense because the archetypes, brought up to date, will appear as the most evident and newest expression of the environment that has conditioned the artist" (1).

Although *Le Passager du transatlantique* does not really fulfill the promise of its first poem, so far as innovative use of verbs is concerned, verbs in this collection already assert Péret's independence of literary poetic tradition. Without having to bear the burden of human feeling or to take on symbolic function, aspects of the everyday world are set at liberty to respond to their own motivation and to follow their own interests.

II *The World Turned Upside Down*

Advancing into the world evoked by Péret's poetry, we come to identify in germination just the first essential step in a process that brings forms to life. Whether these forms be familiar or without analogy in habitual reality, they are invested with remarkable vitality. Thus, in Péret's verse animism demonstrates that features of the real world we are accustomed to consider invariably inanimate—and therefore subject to human control, existing only for man's needs—possess both a will of their own and the ability to act upon, and react to, one another, in a universe where, perforce, man sees his superiority to material things, animal and vegetable forms, violently disputed.

In Péret's writings verbs that serve to breathe life into the physical world are not, strictly speaking, anthropomorphic agents. They endow inanimate things with the will and the power to act, certainly, but not just so that nature can mimic man's behavior. On the contrary, such verbs introduce an ironic note, as they show nonhuman characters, which dominate the action in Péret's poems, parodying human conduct and response. Indian ink puts on its hat of salt butter (II, 266). The threadbare pavement is lost in conjecture about a sun dial made of bread crumbs (II, 46). The skin of a sick stag grieves like a coal mine (I, 87).

Windows suffer from stomach-ache (II, 57). A turnip leans gallantly over blossoming cherry trees (II, 105). Periwinkles shamelessly show their thighs (II, 56). The sleep of trees excites lustful waves (II, 147). Ash, "the sickness of cigars," imitates concierges coming downstairs (I, 182). A portmanteau makes fun of a little cockchafer lost in the desert where ham nearly dies of hunger (II, 40).

Among verbs of the kind illustrated above a few are worthy of special notice, since they recur several times. Puddings cry out (II, 81). So, "like enraged sauerkraut," does the finger of a glove (II, 155). Other improbable beings—frosted-glass spectacles (II, 85), rusty armor (II, 271), oysters (I, 202), and coal (I, 59)—all sing, as do the buttons on a jacket, just before going off arm in arm with sailors (II, 89). Meanwhile, a clock persists in laughing before it strikes, "to signify to its owners that the world is turned upside down" (II, 33). Laughter is just as much the privilege of hills (II, 95). And yet, in spite of its capacity for enjoyment, the external world is no less subject to boredom than man. Old clocks yawn in sardine cans (II, 44). Chinese lanterns of felt yawn "like haricot beans" (II, 32) and billiard tables "like locomotives" (II, 108). Its feet entangled in its hair, collodion is "bored bored bored like a bunch of lilies in a suitcase" (I, 205).

Out of context—or rather, in the context of everyday living—verbs like *cry, laugh,* and *weep* would appear unexceptionable. It is the displacement they undergo in Péret's verse that causes them to resist reasonable assimilation. Here animating verbs set up a barrier between the familiar world and the one sustained by poetic invention. Whereas traditionally the anthropomorphic image makes nature a prisoner of man, Péret's verbs guarantee the natural universe, and those elements of it that incite the poet to imaginative creation, an independence that can be measured by reason's inability to relate their conduct to our own. Now objects compete with the animal kingdom for our attention. Almost invariably, meanwhile, man is ousted from the field of poetic activity. For this reason, when we look at verbs that bestow life upon the real and imagined creatures brought to our notice by Péret's poems, we discover we cannot understand simply by interpreting their behavior according to the standards of human conduct that experience of reality has taught us to consider generally applicable.

In this connection, it is helpful to consider a revealing aspect of Péret's poetic imagination. This comes into focus if we begin by looking at a well-known verse borrowed from Guillaume Apollinaire's poem "Zone." Here animism is ensured by a verb that on the surface is more colorful than those that we have just seen Péret favor: "Bergère ô tour Eiffel le troupeau des ponts bêle ce matin" ("Shepherdess oh Eiffel Tower the flock of bridges is bleating this morning"). Apollinaire's line conveys an image that the sensibility has no difficulty assimilating without protest from reason, since the rational mind finds it easy to elucidate. Once we accept the comparison of the Eiffel Tower to a shepherdess, likening Paris bridges over the Seine to sheep follows naturally enough, while extension of the pastoral image needs no other justification than the sound of morning city traffic. No objections present themselves in the reader's mind, because the image successfully reconciles familiar reality with fanciful representation.

It is in this sense that, by the criteria reflected in Péret's poetic practice, Apollinaire's image is merely decorative, doing no more than refer us back to the reality we knew before we began reading "Zone." On the other hand a poem called "Soupe," in *A Tâtons*, allows us to weigh the difference between the fashion in which Apollinaire's imagination worked and the manner in which Péret's did. It begins:

A gauche du canot dont on tire des sons harmonieux
bêle un monticule couronné d'une aile battante
et l'air qu'elle brasse gémit
plante saisonnière condamnée par les mois en r
enduit de confiture des pieds à la tête

To the right of the rowboat from which harmonious sounds
                                                    are extracted
bleats a hillock crowned by a flapping wing
and the air it stirs up moans
a seasoned plant condemned by the months with an r in them
coated from head to foot with jam

(II, 197)

In Péret action and interaction takes us not into the *Zone*—the outskirts of the French capital—but into the zone of the inexplicable, where the steaming nostrils of the heavenly empire prowl around faded flowers (I, 55), where a pretty woman's breasts watch the slow flight of postage stamps (II, 268), and where the timid smile of new caps, traveling in the shadows, watch passing closed shutters that have never thought about the misfortunes of snakes crouching in front of gateways (I, 137).

In the zone of the inexplicable, commonplace verbs that elsewhere would not detain us an instant present insurmountable obstacles to rational acceptance. A navel goes downstairs without worrying about whether rain is falling (II, 71). White wine plays hide and seek with the tails of pigs one meets everyday in hotel corridors (II, 62). In other words, the wildly improbable characters that move through the poems of Péret engage in acts that, when they are the ones carrying these out, in the places where they find themselves by habit or accident of circumstance, strike us as at least unlikely and sometimes as quite unthinkable. In drizzling rain, a snowdrop accosts naked women as they pass by (II, 35). Meeting the cool wind, nipples bid it good-day (II, 71). Brutal chance is provoked by the meeting on a staircase of bottles between an orange and a key ring, and between the moment when flow becomes ebb and a hanged man's slip knot (I, 56). An old suitcase, a sock, and endive make an appointment to meet between two blades of grass growing out of an altar where intestines live (II, 41). A few rectangular stones arrange to get together on the tongue of a fireman who, for the occasion, imagines himself to be an oak tree (II, 36). A tower, increasing in length, and a dog, dragging its tail the way a garden drags its flower bed along, meet in a dentist's waiting room (II, 94).

III *Words That Make Love*

In Péret's poems, encounters—improbable or even altogether inconceivable in a reasonably ordered world—between animated objects that unaccountably meet in unlikely places, for purposes unexplained, follow a pattern repeated often enough to become persuasive evidence that, like other Surrealists of the first generation, Benjamin Péret fell under the influence of Lautréamont. In Péret's case, there is no occasion to speak, necessarily, of conscious imitation, as with Breton and Soupault, writing their play *Vous m'oublierez*.[2] All the same, there seems every reason to suppose that, like others among the original Surrealists, Péret acknowledged in a comparison from Lautréamont's *Les Chants de Maldoror* that they all knew by heart—"beautiful as the fortuitous encounter in a dissecting table of a sewing-machine and an umbrella"—the succinct expression of a revolutionary ideal of beauty that would serve Surrealism in its revolt against inherited aesthetic criteria. In *Dormir, dormir dans les pierres* we find two comparisons that distinctly echo Lautréamont's: "beautiful as a hole in a window pane" and "beautiful as the unexpected encounter of a cataract and a bottle" (I, 60). Péret's lifelong devotion to the principle of revolt in the area of poetic activity is confirmed in one of his last poems, "La braise à face de portefaix dépenaillé," written in 1959. Here no less than eighteen unrelated elements—material objects like a soup bowl, intangibles like the north wind, and elusive phenomena like "the adverb casting envious glances"— all make an appointment to meet on a night "full of bewildered dust" (II, 309).

The process by which such encounters are projected has been defined quite appositely by Max Ernst, who fittingly alluded to Lautréamont when explaining the meaning of pictorial collage in Surrealism. Admitting that collage had been practiced before the Surrealists came along, as "the cutting up of various flat reproductions of objects or of parts of objects and the pasting of these together to form a picture of something new or old," Ernst went on to argue that Surrealism has so systematized and modified certain procedures, collage among them, that "it is now possible to photograph either on paper or on canvas the amazing graphic appearance of thoughts and desires." Citing "the celebrated Lautréamont quotation" next, Ernst paraphrased it when saying collage "amounts to the exploiting of *the fortuitous encounter upon a nonsuitable plane of two mutually distant realities*," or, "to use a more handy expression, the cultivation of the effects of a *systematic putting out of place*."[3] Less clumsily, in Dorothea Tanning's translation, a revised version of the same statement reads, "I am tempted to see in collage the exploitation of the chance meeting of two distant realities on an unfamiliar plane, or, to use a shorter term, the culture of systematic displacement and its effects."[4]

The pertinence of these remarks to the verbal equivalent of pictorial collage is not difficult to grasp. Nor is this unexpected, when we recall that Ernst is the man who conceived of the *phallustrade*: a balustrade with just a touch of phallus. True enough, in Péret's automatic practice Ernst's technique is not subject to systematic application. Even so, Péret's poems present results that meet the criterion set down in Ernst's "Beyond Painting": "THE MIRACLE OF THE TOTAL TRANSFIGURATION OF BEINGS AND OBJECTS WITH OR WITHOUT MODIFICATION OF THEIR PHYSICAL OR ANATOMICAL ASPECT" (12).

Already we have heard Ernst refer to desire, in connection with the birth of collage. Now, in a more detailed analysis of the process by which a collage comes into existence, he goes further still. In "Beyond Painting" he emphatically links the notion of desire with the idea of lovemaking. "A ready-made reality," which seems to have a function fixed once and for all (a canoe), finding itself in the presence of "another and hardly less absurd reality" (a vacuum cleaner), in a place where both of them "must feel displaced" (a forest), will, "by this very fact, escape its naive destination and its identity." This is to say, according to Ernst, "it will pass from its false absolute, through a series of relative values, into a new absolute value, true and poetic: canoe and vacuum cleaner will make love" (13). With this comment, Max Ernst sends us back once again to Benjamin Péret's observations in *Le Déshonneur des poètes* and his *Anthologie de l'Amour sublime*. For it is there, as our examination of Péret's conjunctions has shown, that poetry is equated with desire, through which, we are told, the marvelous finds its true outlet in love. Ernst does this, interestingly, in a manner that calls to mind two memorable phrases with which André Breton closed an early essay that laid the foundation of the poetic use of language in Surrealism: "Words anyway have stopped playing" and "Words make love."[5]

Nothing illustrates better than Péret's use of verbs the Surrealist concept of poetic language as generative. And nothing dramatizes the generative nature of Surrealist poetic language better than the act of coupling exemplified in the strange encounters that impress themselves upon our attention everywhere in his verse.

In quite a literal sense, desire holds our attention at every turn, in Péret's poetic universe. Sighs "climb the vine-props of desire four at a time" (II, 204). The swelling of a river predisposes its dark banks to desires no less dark (I, 191). Indeed, desire knows no commonsensical limitations here. A star wants nylon stockings (I, 178). A court of law wants to fish for toes in a plate of sauce and, incidentally, pays the price of its desire: drowning (II, 50). *Dernier Malheur, dernière chance* speaks of "satisfying a desire more vast than all the horizons" (II, 156). Moreover, just as desire is limitless, so is the capacity to seek and effect its satisfaction. An accordion mentioned in *Le Grand Jeu* could have devoured earth and bird life, "if it had felt like it" (I, 81).

More interesting, all the same, are those forms of desire that express a deep-rooted need for change—angora spiders that would like to change into a dress so as to "mold a joyous body of sea" (II, 154), or the rotting accordion—not the self-confident one mentioned a moment ago—that, "in the simplicity of its soul," would have liked to be a horse (I, 80). For this expression of desire points directly to a potent force at work everywhere in Péret's verse: the metamorphic principle.

IV   *"The Unknown Rustling of Sudden Metamorphoses"*

Reading Benjamin Péret, one must be prepared to see his poetry, from one moment to the next, "extract the unknown rustling of sudden metamorphoses" (II, 249). In no small measure, this is because a number of distinctive tendencies characterize those strange creatures his verse brings before us. First, they are not averse to concealing their identity, even though their reasons for doing so are not clear. For example, Péret mentions deepest sighs that camouflage themselves sometimes as baths of milk, "stormy as a sheep," and sometimes as "a thick brute," dreaming of lace "like a haricot bean in the moonlight" (II, 150). Then, too, they participate somewhat less voluntarily in a process of change, as when one thing believes itself to be another. It will take only one more kick in the behind, we are informed, for an empty sardine can to believe itself a saint (II, 100). Such a transformation would not be especially noteworthy, if it were merely a sign of delusion. What gives it importance is that it results from a gift, shared by a number of Péret's nonhuman characters, for making totally unexpected discoveries about themselves. Near "a house of sun and white hair," a forest finds it has both a capacity for tenderness and a skeptical turn of mind (I, 88). And such gifts, we observe, can precipitate startling desires. This is the case, for instance, when a pin suddenly feels the ambition to become a limousine (II, 91). True, water springs hesitate to become camembert cheese (II, 200); but a barber's warm towel is already the sigh a woman makes after love (II, 103).

In every instance, action and reaction are governed by an all-pervading principle of metamorphosis, subject to no restrictions of any kind. The metamorphic principle operates on a wide scale, penetrating well below the surface where, upon occasion, key words pinpoint its effect. Reality is rarely, if ever, static here. And the same is true of the Surreal, as Péret depicts it. Looking at the following extract from a poem called "Picasso," we immediately identify in "devenus brioches" an allusion to change:

> Les fleurs électriques des estomacs pétrifiés par
> des yeux d'Acropole
> les courses en sac des machines recherchant leurs
> outils devenus brioches
> les cauchemars de la bouteille de bière égarée
> dans la forêt
> comme une langouste dans un édredon

> The electric flowers of stomachs petrified by
> Acropolis eyes
> the sack races of machines looking for their tools
> changed into brioches
> the nightmares of the bottle of beer lost in the
> forest
> like a lobster in an eider-down

> (II, 262)

Metamorphosis is not confined to this phrase, however. Each substantive manifests itself before us in turn, only to be subjected without delay to radical transformation under the influence of what follows it, modifying adjective or adjectival phrase. In this process of perpetual recreation, reorientation, and mutation, brought about by the generative action of words, verbs have a capital role: in a sugar-loaf there beats a human heart, which dissolves little by little to form a tear, which, as if on parade, advances over a cheek... (II, 207).

Blue cliffs writhe (I, 170). A soft stone dissolves (II, 279). Porcelain mountains go soft once again (II, 264). Bows drown themselves in a plain so submerged that it is no longer a plain but a hand: "In a little while it will be a belly / then a torso" (I, 200–1). The trend followed by Péret's verse characteristically gives verbs unlimited freedom to effect transformations in the material universe. These verbs do not merely foster instability; they eliminate the possibility of stasis and accelerate change. Hence they hold a prominent position in this extract from *A Tâtons*:

> Couper la lumière en quatre et la jeter aux fauves
> Extraire du sable toutes les dents qui s'y trouvent
> pour en hérisser les murs
> ....
> Brûler les camemberts trops faits jusqu'à ce que le
> phénix s'en échappe
> Battre les tapis avec un rasoir pour fabriquer des
> cages à serins

> Cut light into four and throw it to wild animals
> Extract from sand all the teeth that are there to
> cover the walls with spikes
> ....
> Burn overripe camembert cheeses until the phoenix
> rises from them
> Beat carpets with a razor to make canary cages
>
>   (II, 202)

In the world projected by Péret's imagination, imitation is facilitated because it is possible to ignore the boundaries reason acknowledges to be insurmountable, but which desire is at liberty to ignore. Otherwise, how could the squeaking of axles hope to imitate long meditations (II, 264)? The poet's advice is unequivocal: "Don't hesitate and you'll see the bread's lifeline sliced lengthwise" (II, 313). Once reasonable hesitation is behind us, we can watch verbs break down the distinctions between the tangible and the intangible, the concrete and the ineffable, in a universe where such distinctions are of no significance. We can now see mountains swimming in a sea of light (I, 75), the caresses of snow flies swimming in imploring hair (I, 49), intransitive verbs going mildewy (II, 319), and the daily tide of laughter ebb and flow in a soap factory (II, 261). We can witness, too, the awakening of an energy stammering with tears (II, 171), a tree with no trunk wandering overhead (II, 279), a cloud of dust playing the bugle as it passes over a town, playing so loudly, in fact, that its hat trembles and its beard rises up to bite its nose (II, 28).

V *"Swallows of Words that Open the Morning's Shutters"*[6]

The verb is the vivifying core of the grammatical statement. Neither conjunctions nor prepositions can transport us into the world of the marvelous without the collaboration of verbs. Any weakening, any compromise with mundane reality, manifested through verbal structures, would mark the collapse of everything that conjunctions and prepositions have combined to bring about. Any reluctance evidenced through verbal forms would confine both the preposition and the conjunction to a vacuum, condemning them to imaginative sterility. There is no sign of inconsistency in Péret's writing, however. In all his poems, verbs animate a universe at odds with the world observation has made familiar and science has explained. Verbs permit exploration of situations and description of phenomena that have no counterpart in everyday experience. "The poetry of Péret never stops," Claude Courtot has remarked, "it is a song of incessant qualification" (114). True as this statement is, it calls for expansion, since Péret's verse depicts a world in incessant activity, necessarily relying on verbs in so doing.

In Péret's poems verbs typically exemplify rejection of rationalist evaluations. It is not enough, though, to notice that verbs help the poet challenge the rational. For Péret's verse transcends reason. Because our education has inculcated faith in reason as the key to an understanding of the world in which we live, it is only to be expected that we shall look at Péret's poetry, at first, as a sustained protest against rationalist interpretations. It takes closer acquaintance with his work to reveal that Péret's inclinations as a poet simply ignore the distinction between the reasonable and the unreasonable. To look for deliberate intent behind his poetic practice would mean reducing his poems to the mere demonstration of a theory, painstakingly applied. The sad result would be insensitivity to the creative spontaneity from which his poems draw vitality and freshness.

Péret's writing repeatedly casts the universe loose from the moorings upon which reason counts to immobilize it. When this happens, the central role of the verb in the poetic statement makes possible a confrontation between words that common sense treats as unassociable, so liberating a sense of the marvelous. Verbs do even more when their own ambiguity denies reason its privileges in assessing the visible. In the following lines from *Le Grand Jeu*, interpreting the verb *rouler* places the reasonable mind in a predicament: "La mer de savon / qui roule des cigares neufs" (I, 216). Since a sea of soap and new cigars have nothing in common, on the plane of rational utility, the idea of the former rolling the latter affords common sense no satisfaction. But Péret's theory and practice both rest firmly on the assumption that imagination need not be confined within reasonable projection. Hence the two lines cited here provide imaginative stimulus that is strengthened, not weakened, by the fact that, outside the realm of reason, *rouler* can be read as "cheat," or "beat," just as well as "roll." Asserting its rights, reason may point out that "roll" seems most unlikely, in this instance, because rolling a cigarette is an action that life can give us the opportunity to witness. How, though, does one roll a cigar destined, like the ones of which Benjamin Péret speaks in *Le Grand Jeu*, "for warlike lewdness"?

Benjamin Péret's verbs efficiently release poetry from the obligation to abide by reasonable formulation. In so doing, they play a vital role by showing that, for him, poetic revolution represented something other than an effort to provide a novel intellectual experience or even an unfamiliar emotional one. In his verse the verb quickly takes command of the poetic statement, indicating that poetry rests here on a radical change in sensibility. One poem from *De Derrière les fagots* begins:

> Je m'étonne de l'orthographe de *fois*
> qui ressemble tant à un champignon
> roulé dans la farine

> I'm surprised at the spelling of *times*
> that so resembles a mushroom
> rolled in flour

(II, 39)

As is frequently the case, this text, "Chasse à courre," opens on a verb. Without apology or forewarning, we find ourselves in the realm of the marvelous.

Someone who protests that he can see nothing in the lines reproduced above that is not simply ludicrous will be unlikely to find any statement in Péret's writings capable of changing his opinion. We have to look to another Surrealist, if we wish to find one willing to offer something approaching an explanation for what Péret has done. We may turn, for example, to André Breton, praising subversive works that stand for resistance to general domestication. Then we can see that, with remarkable vigor, Péret has applied the principle defended by Breton, subjecting words themselves to scrutiny, and showing them to be anything but domesticated.

A rationalist's difficulties with Péret begin in earnest when he discovers that, in Péret's eyes, resemblance had nothing to do with observable similarity or commonsense association. Resemblance was to be grasped poetically, being imaginatively projected. In varying degree this was true of all the major Surrealist poets of Péret's generation, for whom Paul Eluard spoke when he declared, in *Donner à voir*, "Everything is comparable to everything, everything finds its echo, its reason, its resemblance, its opposition, its flux everywhere. And this flux is infinite" (134).

Péret never engaged in defense of a principle that gave meaning to the resemblances his poems established in "Chasse à courre," from *De Derrière les fagots*, and "Sans tomates pas d'artichauts," from *Le Grand Jeu*:

> Mes tomates sont plus mûres que tes sabots
> et tes artichauts ressemblent à ma fille

> My tomatoes are riper than your sabots
> and your artichokes resemble my daughter
>
> (I, 227)

He never explained, either, how the gray, blue, green, red oriflammes mentioned in another poem from *Le Grand Jeu* "have the shape of my face / for I have made them like my laughter" (I, 200).

Demonstration takes precedence over theoretical argument, as Péret's verbs function in a way that shows the objective world to be possessed of unlimited possibilities. Hence verbs reveal what things are capable of becoming, of doing, once freed from the necessity to occupy only the place assigned them by reason, in a rationally ordered and comprehensible existence. Benjamin Péret's attention went most frequently to features of physical reality that may seem trivial. All the same, he brought to the examination of the world about him a capacity for wonder, derived from a gift that, in Surrealism, ranks as supremely poetic: the ability to detect analogies that deserve the qualification poetic even though they are inexplicable or inadmissible, on the plane of reasonable verbal exchange.

In his poetic universe very little, as *Un Point c'est tout* proves, separates lamps from nougat forgotten in a drawer. A pipe stem is nothing but a long, rather warm animal's muzzle. A penny is nothing other than an Adam's apple in a strongbox, we find in *De Derrière les fagots* (II, 78). In *Dernier Malheur, dernière chance*, the sound of a trumpet is equated with a warm octopus' tentacle (II, 171). Similarly, the sad glimmer of an oil lamp, mentioned in *A Tâtons*, is a cat, ready to pounce on the breathless scars on a wall (II, 199). How best to describe a stuffed dog, in *De Derrière les fagots*? Certainly not by means of simple comparisons, treated contemptuously in the *Manifeste du surréalisme* (52):

Mais quel chien
On aurait dit une lanterne vénitienne
demandant l'aumône à un chef de gare
une brouette appelant Pascal à la rescousse
un tremblement de terre hésitant entre Naples et Tokio
ou entre le premier et le cinquième étage

But what a dog
You'd have said it was a Chinese lantern
asking alms of a stationmaster
a wheelbarrow calling Pascal to its assistance
an earthquake unable to make up its mind between Naples and Tokyo
or between the first and fifth floors

(II, 36)

The same collection refers to a nude woman, "so white you'd say she was a pine forest / in a keyhole" (II, 110). And "Minute" (1934) speaks of the brain of a newborn child as so sly "you'd say it was a daisy exfoliated by a cockchafer that had come out of a pope's armpit" (II, 266).

It is Breton who provides the theoretical justification for poetic affirmations like these, when he comments on the nature of the image, in his first Surrealist manifesto: "It is from the somewhat fortuitous coming together of the two terms that a particular light has sprung, *the light of the image*, to which we are infinitely sensitive. The value of the image depends on the beauty of the spark produced; it is, consequently, a function of the difference of potential between the two conductors" (52). As for Péret, he offered no additional comments, when he might have insisted, for instance, that the beauty of the spark is increased, the farther apart the two potentials are located. So far as he ever took the trouble to explain himself, he did so when he expressed confidence in poetry as being, to borrow a phrase from his *Anthologie des Mythes*, "as natural to man as seeing and sleeping."

CHAPTER 8

Love: Je sublime *and* Un Point c'est tout

I   *"Poetry, Geometric Place of Love and Revolt"*[1]

TO readers acquainted with no more of Péret's verse than has helped illustrate how evocation of the marvelous makes special demands upon verbs, prepositions, and conjunctions, it might seem logical to infer that, of all the Surrealist writers, Benjamin Péret would have been the least inclined to write love poems. His work manifests clear preference for a mode of poetic communication apparently finding little or no impetus in private emotion. Moreover, except in his narrative texts he evidently tended to situate poetic experience in a world where, for the most part, human beings are but accessory figures. And he obviously continued throughout his life to be reticent on the subject of events in which he had been involved personally. For these reasons, Péret certainly looks to have been less well equipped than several of his contemporaries in Surrealism to make room for love in his poetry: the contrast his temperament presents with that of Breton, Desnos, and Eluard is especially striking in this respect. If his poetic practice were to support this hypothesis, then Péret's place among the first-generation Surrealist writers would be that of an exception who turned his back upon one of the richest sources of Surrealist inspiration.

The first Surrealists were quick to realize that nothing so readily and so persistently as love stimulates opposition to the pressures applied by society, in demanding of all men uniformity in thought and conformity in behavior. To André Breton and his companions, love seemed at once deserving of particular attention, as one of the purest and most vital expressions of the outlaw spirit that gives individual man purpose and direction, leading him to define and pursue his needs beyond socially accepted limits. This is why Breton himself declared categorically,

120

with respect to man's situation in the modern world, that there is no solution outside love. In any Surrealist, indifference to love would mean being incapable of participating in one of the most fruitful of Surrealism's programs of revolt. And it would mean, most certainly, foregoing the chance to explore the marvelous to the fullest extent.

We know that Benjamin Péret was totally dedicated to the task of uncovering evidence of the marvelous potential of existence. Hence ignoring love would have made sense to him only if he had been unable to experience it. Already, though, we have heard him testify to the central role assumed by desire, in that revolutionary act he called poetry. So it is no sign of inconsistency that we find him speaking of love in numerous poems. Here the name of Rosa and the initial *H* discreetly conceal the identity of the woman or women who had prompted him to adopt a perspective on reality in no way conflicting with all we have discovered in his work so far. It is just as consonant with his practice that Péret should have set forth his ideas on love, *l'amour sublime*, in a preface to an anthology of other men's writings, rather than in a foreword to one of his own verse collections devoted to love, *Je sublime* (1936) and *Un Point c'est tout* (1946).[2] Making due allowances for temperamental differences—Breton, for example, preferred to speak of *l'amour fou*—Benjamin Péret's preface to his *Anthologie de l'Amour sublime* of 1956 demonstrated the orthodoxy of his views, in the context of Surrealism.[3] At the same time, this substantial essay fully guaranteed its author the right to make an original contribution to the Surrealist treatment of love.

It is no secret that the Surrealists—who dedicated to Eros their 1959–1960 international exhibition in Paris—have evinced an abiding interest in eroticism. While Robert Desnos' essay *De l'Erotisme*, published posthumously in 1952, was written especially for the wealthy bibliophile Jacques Doucet, the *Lexique succinct de l'érotisme* compiled by a number of Surrealists in 1970 clearly was not a commissioned work. In spite of the fact that Surrealists have expressed unyielding abhorrence before all forms of titillation in literature and art, their preoccupation with the erotic still can lend itself to misinterpretation. At one extreme, it is true, their interest seems simple to explain:

Paul Eluard's passion for collecting dirty postcards, shall we say.[4]
And there does seem to be some justification for believing that
the Surrealist practice of eroticism can scarcely be distinguished
from pornography, when it takes the provocative form adopted
by Aragon and Péret in their *1929*, suitably illustrated by the
Surrealist photographer Man Ray. All the same, the intent of
Aragon's pseudonymously published narrative of 1928, *Le Con
d'Irène,* is not exploitive.[5] This text fits the description of
eroticism to be found in Aragon's *Le Paysan de Paris*: "an
outlaw principle, an irrepressible sense of violation, contempt
for prohibition, and taste for confusion." The same may be
said of Desnos' *La Papesse du diable* which appeared only in
1958, under the unlikely fictitious names of Jehan Sylvius and
Pierre de Ruynes. These are, significantly, two works of Surrealist protest in which eroticism is a typical sign of social and
moral nonconformity, as is also, despite the fact that it includes
the poems he printed in *1929*, a work that Benjamin Péret wrote
in 1928, *Les Couilles enragées.*

In some ways, *Les Couilles enragées* is an exceptional example
of Péret's writing, just as the line drawings contributed anony-
mously by Yves Tanguy are exceptional in the work of that
Surrealist painter. Nevertheless, it calls for a brief analysis, if we
are to approach the question of love, as reflected in Péret's
poetry.

With every justification, its publisher claimed that *Les Couilles
enragées,* in which prose and verse passages alternate, escapes
the limitations that usually weigh upon publications of no more
than prurient interest.[6] This is largely because, in defiance of
social and moral norms, it testifies to the influence of a lively
imagination easy for us to identify by now: "from behind the
drapes rose the most beautiful legs in the world and moans
capable on their own of transforming mica into car driver's
goggles" (10). Who else but Benjamin Péret would have said
such a thing? Who else would have commented, apropos of a
watch being vigorously employed by an onanist blonde, "But
the watch, which wasn't accustomed to being used for this
purpose, didn't know which way to look..." (11)?

By and large, though, the imaginative harvest is not bountiful
in *Les Couilles enragées.* Particularly in the verse sections, where

vulgarity discourages quotation, one feels, despite the fact that
Péret's imagination functions in the way we have become accustomed to seeing it do, that it is inhibited by acceptance of a
dominant theme—masturbation or sodomy, for instance—that im-
poverishes imaginative play, canalizing its effects. The result is
interestingly similar to what we find in "Toute une vie," the verse
tribute that Péret dedicated to André Breton. In both cases, we
have the distinct impression that the current of poetic energy
has been reduced by the poet's wish to follow out a theme he
intends to develop in a sustained manner. In Benjamin Péret,
imaginative activity was most fruitful when it benefited from the
spontaneity to which automatism promised access.

The degree of poetic intensity attained in *Je sublime* and
Un Point c'est tout significantly sets these publications apart
from *Les Couilles enragées*. Yet this is not the most important
difference separating the verse collections in question from the
earlier work. In fact, *Les Couilles enragées* is really worthy of
mention in connection with Péret's treatment of love only because
of the sharp contrast it presents in relation to its author's attitude
toward love.

A noteworthy feature of love, as depicted in Péret's verse, is
the way it illustrates "the complete abandon without which no
true love is conceivable," according to his *Anthologie de l'Amour
sublime* (8). This form of abandon entails surrender of all
restraints upon the language used to speak of love. Yet it does
not find characteristic expression through vulgarity or indecency.
Liberation from social and moral inhibitions leads the poet
through automatism, not into obscenity, but into a mode of
discourse that ignores rational limitations. As a consequence,
Péret's love poems communicate a sense of wonder that carries
the reader directly into the realm of the marvelous, instead
of into the conventional world of the literary erotic.

An isolated experiment, to which nothing suggests that Péret
attached special importance, *Les Couilles enragées* stands at
the opposite pole from those poems in which he addressed himself to the subject of love. Indeed, it is more exact to say of
Benjamin Péret that far more exclusively than Breton or Eluard—
who both alluded openly to sexual encounter in their love
poems—he concerned himself with the effect of love, rather than

with its physical expression, characteristically translating his impressions into a highly personal view of the world about him.

II *Love that Sexualizes the Universe*

It must seem that Péret's handling of the theme of love will be less revolutionary than that of his contemporaries in Surrealism, that there will be nothing in his writings to compare either with the work of later Surrealist poets like Mayoux and Joyce Mansour, or with that of a graphic artist like Bellmer or a painter like Molinier. If this were to turn out to be true, however, it could only be because Benjamin Péret had proved unfaithful, in practice, to his theoretical conception of the role of desire—as expressed through sublime love—summed up in these words from his *Anthologie de l'Amour sublime*: "Desire, in sublime love, far from losing from sight the flesh-and-blood person who has given it birth, tends therefore, finally, to sexualize the universe" (22).

We must take care not to be misled. Sublime love, as Péret spoke of it, is not to be confused with divine love. In "Toute une vie" he praises Breton for bringing love out of "the dark caverns oozing brains foul with incense." As he does throughout his work, in the *Anthologie de l'Amour sublime* he celebrates "the double aspect of sublime love, at once carnal and spiritual" (19). The preface to this anthology stresses that, the Surrealist revolt having been occasioned by the conditions imposed on love by the world and by man, one of the great tasks Surrealism has set itself in the domain of love is "rehabilitation of the flesh, recognized in all its splendor," without which "the very notion of sublime love fades away" (67). While he judged religious myths to have stressed *consolation* over *exaltation*, Péret saw sublime love as "the only myth of pure exaltation," emanating from the very heart of desire and aiming at its full satisfaction. This is why, in his estimation, the marvelous loses its supernatural, extraterrestrial character, taking on definition as it does within the limits of human existence (20). In sublime love, mind, flesh, and heart become one (9). Hence sexualizing the universe did not mean to Péret weighing it down with interpretable references to erotic passion. It meant charging the physical world with desire, so that everything, now, calls for evaluation from the standpoint of desire.

Reality is not invested with symbolic value, to be routinely *translated* into sexual terms. In order to do that, Péret would have had to forsake his firmest convictions, indulging in a process of intellectualization quite alien to his creative personality. Far more characteristic of his response to love, and so much more in keeping with his conception of poetry, is the first poem of *Dormir, dormir dans les pierres*. Here, implicitly asking how he knows he is in love, the poet takes no account of literary tradition, exploits none of the stock emotional responses. Love is signaled by a sense of reality as marvelous:

Si l'amour naît de la projection d'une groseille dans le bec d'un cygne
j'aime
car le cygne de mon sang a mangé toutes les groseilles du monde
car le monde n'est que groseilles
et les groseilles du monde jaillissent de ses yeux
comme le sel des arbres
comme l'eau des mains sonores
et comme les caresses des mouches de neige
nageant le soir sur les cheveux défaits qui les implorent

If love is born of the thrusting of a currant into the beak of a swan
I'm in love
for my blood's swan has eaten all the currants in the world
for the world is nothing but currants
and the currants of the world burst from its eyes
like salt from trees
like water from sonorous hands
and like caresses from snow flies
swimming in the evening over beseeching disheveled hair

(I, 49)

In these lines, the interdependence of love and the marvelous finds sustained illustration. Love becomes manifest when the physical universe is marvelously transformed. Meanwhile, the marvelous is testimony to the presence of love, as the natural environment undergoes changes that, being rationally inexplicable, bear witness to the wonder of love.

Love poems offer a special interest in Péret's work, but not

because they celebrate the beauty of woman in a conventionally
descriptive manner. For, as we are advised in the *Anthologie de
l'Amour sublime*, woman is beautiful, in Péret's eyes, "to the
extent that she incarnates more completely the secret aspirations
of man, inciting him to turn over full power to his faculties of
sublimation" (70). Péret is saying essentially the same thing
as Breton, who in *Arcane 17* spoke of woman as assisting man
in overcoming "opacity," when he declares love to be the "only
fully sacred" human feeling.[7] This is why Péret's poems of love
do not analyze his feelings in an effort to communicate his
excitement. Instead, they detail his strange relations with an
exterior universe in which that excitement is reflected:

> Nue nue comme ma maîtresse
> la lumière descend le long de mes os
> et les scies du temps grincent leur chanson de charbon
> car le charbon chante aujourd'hui
> le charbon chante comme un liquide d'amour
>
> Nude nude like my mistress
> light moves down along my bones
> and the saws of time whine their song of coal
> for coal sings today
> coal sings like a liquid of love

                                                            (I, 59)

Franklin Rosemont comments appositely in his *Radical America*
article: "It must be emphasized that Péret is, far more than is
generally thought, a poet of love. But love for Péret has nothing
to do with conventional pseudo-amorous sentimentality nor with
the vile platitudes of so-called 'popular' music: it is, rather, the
most decisive and thoroughgoing individual human experience,
comprising the most delirious and overpowering moments of
one's life: love which is wild, succulent, corrosive, frenzied,
violently opposed to the last shred of Christian morality and
to every other conceivable social constraint; love which, in a
single glance, is capable of reinventing, from scratch, one's
conception of life" (7).
Even when Péret's language comes closest to traditional usage,
it nevertheless bears the imprint of an original sense of the world

transformed. Thus allusions to the parts of a woman's body lead somewhere quite different from where we might expect the evocation of sensual experience to be taking us; in *Un Point c'est tout*, for instance:

> J'ai tellement tes seins dans ma poitrine
> que deux cratères fumants s'y dessinent comme un
> renne dans une caverne
> pour te recevoir comme l'armure reçoit la femme nue
> attendue du fond de sa rouille
> en se liquéfiant comme les vitres d'une maison qui brûle
> comme un château dans une grande cheminée

> I have your breasts so much in my chest
> that two smoking craters take form there like a
> reindeer in a cave
> to receive you as armor receives the nude woman
> awaited from deep in its rust
> liquifying like the panes of a burning house
> like a castle in a great fireplace

(II, 184)

Péret's commitment to communicating the marvelous made it seem natural to pass through private feeling into depiction of the universe that feelings made accessible to him. This, indeed, is the value of feeling, that it becomes a pathway, leading in his poems to revelations about the world which could not be attained so easily without its assistance. Hence the process of sexualizing the universe is accompanied by another, having the complementary effect of transfiguring sexuality. The preface to the *Anthologie de l'Amour sublime* describes this second process in precise detail: "Recognizing the universality of desire, its cosmic significance and its manifestations in man calls at the same time for its sublimation and that of the object of this desire. While outside sublime love the human being—especially man—scarcely abandons himself to love, except in the measure that he reduces desire to its most primitive state, in sublime love beings caught in its vertigo aspire only to letting themselves be carried as far as possible from this state. Desire, while still being linked with sexuality, then sees itself transformed" (20).

No one can understand the excitement that love brought Benjamin Péret while yet ignoring the sexual aspect of passion. However, no real progress is possible, either, unless one appreciates that the excitement love brought him transcended the limitations of sexual satisfaction.

III *Love as a Revolutionary Force*

Surrealists speak about no subject with greater uniformity than about love. All the same, the effect of general agreement among them is anything but one of monotony. They are witnesses to a profound and fascinating conviction: faith in woman as mediatrix between man and the universe of desire, the realm of the marvelous. In the circumstances, it would be an error to look to Benjamin Péret for a viewpoint unparalleled in the writings of other Surrealists. On the contrary, the first step toward appreciation of what Péret's love poems have to offer is understanding the role with which Surrealist convictions invest the sexual partner.

Citing the *Tao*—"Heaven and earth being united together, dew falls softly"—Péret comments in his *Anthologie de l'Amour sublime*, "It is indeed on this perfect complementarity, intuitively perceived, that sublime love rests, and it is from possession of the complementary person that mutual happiness results" (10). With this affirmation goes another: "Contradictory impulsions are incompatible with sublime love which, it so happens, presupposes their reconcilement in perfect accord" (17). This is why Péret goes on to define sublime love as "that perfect accord between two people harmoniously matched" (23). It explains why sublime love is represented in his anthology as "'asocial and sometimes even antisocial." These ideas fuse, in one poem from *Un Point c'est tout*, in this typical image: "'for without you I am scarcely the chink between the paving stones of imminent barricades" (II, 183).

It is not through inciting man to feel dissatisfied with the world about him that love becomes a revolutionary force in Surrealism. Rather, love is revolutionary when it reveals the transitory nature of so much in physical reality that modern man takes to be proof of the stability of that world, where desires are circumscribed, not to say stifled, by the laws and customs of society. As a celebration of the revelations love brings, Péret's love poems are a standing invitation to revolt; in *Le Grand Jeu,* for instance:

> Parfois une femme au regard courbe
> m'offrait son sein ferme comme une pomme
> Alors j'étais pendant des jours et des jours
> sans revoir la nuit et ses poissons
> Alors j'allais par les champs de jambes de femme
> cueillir la neige et les liquides odorantes
> dont j'oignais mes oreilles
> afin de percevoir le bruit que font les mésanges en mourant

> Sometimes a woman with curved glance
> would offer me her breast firm as an apple
> Then I went for days and days
> without again seeing night and its fish
> Then I'd pass through fields of women's legs
> to gather snow and sweet-smelling liquids
> which I'd rub into my ears
> so as to detect the sound titmice make dying

(I, 179)

Far from preaching revolution, Péret inculcated revolt. His love poems embody a sense of liberation, rather than argue in favor of freedom. They exemplify rejection of controls, regulations, and restrictions, instead of urging us to practice it. And they succeed in this because of the salutary effect of love upon Peret's sensibility. In *Je sublime,* the magical name of Rosa inspires the following words:

> droit comme un mât de cocagne dont j'atteindrai le sommet
> pour que tu me regardes non comme un kilo de sucre
> mais comme une nuit que tu as décousue

> straight as a greasy pole that I'll reach the top of
> so you'll look upon me not as a kilo of sugar
> but as a night you have ripped apart

(II, 133)

In accordance with one of the most vital traditions of Surrealism—one that he himself contributed much to establishing—
Péret's verse, just like Breton's and Eluard's, casts woman in
the fascinating role of mediatrix between man and the marvelous
by presenting a succession of highly original arresting effects.
At one extreme, these incite our physical senses to heightened
acuity. At the other, they confront the senses with evidence
for which lived experience has not prepared us: the sight of a
tree, for example, felled by the perfume of a red-headed
woman (I, 179).

Under the influence of Rosa's magic,

> demain jaillira du désert comme une oasis flottante
> où les pierres crient à tue-tête
> je t'ai vu drapeau de charbon aux étoiles bleues

> tomorrow will burst forth from the desert like a floating oasis
> where the stones cry out at the top of their lungs
> I've seen you flag of coal with blue stars

(I, 131)

The woman to whom the poem "Ecoute" is dedicated can change
days of the week into a fly, on a square lined with ruined
castles from which emerges an immense vegetation of coral and
embroidered shawls (I, 132). Sights no less strange can be
seen in "A H" (II, 142–43). Like the two other texts cited,
"A H" belongs to *Je sublime*, a sequence of sixteen poems,
written between January and March of 1935, representative of
Péret's love poems. Later *Un Point c'est tout* will add its testimony to the mediative function of woman. In "Je ne veux pas"
(II, 187), Péret remains true to his faith in woman, even when
approaching the important question of man's dependence upon
his sexual partner from a negative standpoint, stressing the sad
consequences of her absence in texts like "Un Matin" ("for you
are no more there than I am there without you / and the world
is all disheveled" [II, 186]) and "Pour ne rien dire" (II, 189).
As a late poem, "Les Mains dans les poches" (August, 1959),
confirms with its image of open strongboxes filled with "the light
breath / of resolved enigmas" (II, 314), woman never ceased
to hold for Benjamin Péret the promise of opening up reality
to the marvelous.

In Péret's work woman is everywhere an object of wonder, not just for what she is but also for what she enables the poet to see. She is the wonderful intermediary, without whom the world never would appear so admirably transformed. And so when Péret's poems speak of love, they insistently reiterate unwavering trust in the marvelous as excitingly projected by desire, never remotely unattainable, always accessible through fulfillment of desire, which may be "simple as a salad rising above the tall trees" (II, 136). In the measure that in all Péret's writings it is a celebration of aspirations achieved, desire satisfied, poetry thus raises the "terrible interdict" to which Breton referred. In Péret's ears,

l'écho de ta voix de fantôme de mica marin
répète indéfiniment ton nom
qui ressemble tant au contraire d'une éclipse du soleil
que je me crois quand tu me regardes
un pied d'alouette dans une glacière dont tu ouvrirais la porte
avec l'espoir d'en voir s'échapper une hirondelle de pétrole enflammé

the echo of your ghostly voice of marine mica
indefinitely repeats your name
that so resembles the opposite of an eclipse of the sun
that I believe myself to be when you look at me
a skylark's foot in an icehouse the door of which you open
with the hope of seeing a swallow of flaming kerosene escape

(II, 129)

IV *Love and Convulsive Beauty*

As we consider the kinds of images through which Péret shares with us the wondrous revelations that woman's mediative role makes possible, it soon becomes evident that the task of characterizing their distinctive nature will take us farther than simple realization that literary cliché and emotional stereotype have no place in Péret's writing. Progress beyond negative terms calls for closer examination of the language of love, as employed by Péret. It confronts us at once with a sense of beauty, distinctly Surrealist in quality, that no one has described better than Breton did when, first at the end of *Nadja* and then in a 1942 essay on Max Ernst, he announced, "Beauty will be CONVULSIVE or will not exist."

If we begin with Breton's *L'Amour fou* (1937) we discover that the meaning of the adjective "convulsive" in Surrealist usage is to be sought by way of an examination of the relationship existing between a person in love and the object of his passion. As Breton speaks of it, then, convulsive love is guaranteed by what he calls "circumstantial magic": circumstances entering into magical relationship with one another, under the influence of desire. Needless to say, Breton's dominant preoccupation throughout his *L'Amour fou* is shared by Surrealists in general and by Péret in particular: the question of the relationship of objectivity to subjectivity. Péret's special contribution lies in the manner in which his love poems establish that relationship and sustain it in defiance of reasonable anticipation.

When we compare these texts with other verses of his, no radical departure can be observed in Péret's love poems, under the heading either of substance, of mood, or of viewpoint. What happens is that love brings the poem into focus, centralizing the marvelous, so to speak. As a result, *Je sublime* and *Un Point c'est tout* present a greater unity than any of Péret's other collections. And yet the unity of individual poems of love is not merely of the kind that quickly comes to attention thanks to the use of vocatives that orient feeling and imagery toward the object of the writer's affection. Sentiment is less important, really, than imaginative activity that finds its unifying element when its source comes into focus. In "Clin d'œil" and "Source," from *Je sublime*, Rosa's name figures as a refrain. It makes its appearance only at the end of "A Quand," however. The poem "Je" also mentions it just at the very end: "Rosa is there." As for "Allo," this poem illustrates the function of love in a way excellently illuminating convulsive love, as Péret responded to it.

The first sixteen lines of this poem are characterized by repeated use of the first-person possessive:

Mon avion en flammes mon château inondé de vin du Rhin
mon ghetto d'iris noirs mon oreille de cristal
mon rocher dévalant la falaise pour écraser le garde-champêtre

My flaming plane my castle soaked in Rhenish wine
my ghetto of black irises my ear of crystal
my rock running down the cliff to crush the village policeman

(II, 124)[8]

"My" recurs no less than twenty-six times, without for all that
persuading the reader of the unity of the text before his eyes.
It is as though "Allo" were subject to the effects of an inexplicable centrifugal force, having no identifiable center. Only
when the poem reaches its climax in the disarmingly simple
statement "je t'aime" does one realize that it actually centers
upon an unnamed woman, whom the poet has been trying to
describe. More exactly, we should say, he has been trying to
communicate his response to her, doing so in a manner that
prompts Mary Ann Caws to comment in *The Inner Theatre of
Recent French Poetry*, on a comparable poem, "Clin d'œil" (II,
125), "Unlike the woman described by a normal linguistic
pattern in Breton's famous poem 'L'Union libre' ("Ma femme
aux yeux de savane..."), Rosa is not described as *having*
shoulders of champagne: she is *of* morning opal, etc. Breton's
catalog of attributes is very different from Péret's perception of
coalescence. It is as if there were a certain comfortable distance,
a breathing space, among the elements of Breton's universe,
between the poet and the woman, the woman and her qualities.
Péret's poetry leaves none, since the poet himself wakes up
through her eyes, and since she is literally part of that which
in most poems she would only resemble" (89–90). Another
poem from *Je sublime*, "Source," leaves us with the same
impression:

Il fait un temps Rosa avec un vrai soleil de Rosa
et je vais boire Rosa en mangeant Rosa
jusqu'à ce que je m'endorme d'un sommeil de Rosa
vêtu de rêves Rosa
et l'aube Rosa me réveillera comme un champignon Rosa
où se verra l'image de Rosa entourée d'un halo Rosa

It is Rosa weather with a real sun of Rosa
and I'm going to drink Rosa eating Rosa
until I fall into a sleep of Rosa

dressed in Rosa dreams
and Rosa dawn will awaken me like a Rosa mushroom
in which the image of Rosa will be seen surrounded by a Rosa halo
(II, 138)

We can take Mrs. Caws's comments a little further, then, in the direction that the preface to the *Anthologie de l'Amour sublime* invites us to follow. Here, noting that all myths reflect "man's ambivalence before the world and before himself," and asserting that this ambivalence results from a profound feeling of dissociation inherent in man's nature, Péret comments that man sees himself as "weak and helpless, facing natural forces that dominate him" (19). Hence for Péret the important thing about myths is that they represent an aspiration toward happiness while yet acknowledging the obstacles that stand between man and his desire (20). In other words, the myth of sublime love takes on special value, in Péret's eyes, because it represents the overthrow of those very obstacles and, in the achievement of desire, the elimination of the distressing sense of ambivalence that makes nature seem an alien presence. Love, then, permits the poet to take possession of nature, to assimilate it, to make it part of his joyous celebration of passionate fulfillment. Hence lines like the following, from "Attendre" in *Je sublime,* are of the most profound significance in voicing Péret's triumph over the restrictions from which love has brought release:

la fontaine d'éclairs de mer
engendrée par ton regard où volent d'impalpables papillons de nuit

the fountain of sea lightning
begotten by your glance in which impalpable night butterflies fly
(II, 126)

At first sight, it is images that convey a mood of violence which seem best to exemplify in Péret's love poetry the convulsive quality of Surrealist antisentimental love. And there are plenty of these in *Je sublime*: the flaming plane and downward rolling stone of "Allo," the lava endlessly reproducing the loved one's face in "Je ne dors pas" (II, 129), her image revolving in the poet's head "like a heliotrope maddened by sea

sickness" ("Nébuleuse" [II, 139]), comparison of Rosa's eyes to
a tree with its throat cut in "Le Carré de l'hypoténuse" (II, 134),
the "breasts of explosion" mentioned in "Clin d'œil," and "the
sparrow-hawks of your glances," fishing all "the sardines of my
head," in "Homard" (II, 123). Shifting attention to *Un Point
c'est tout,* we find two poems to be particularly rich in images
of a similar nature: "Sais-tu" (II, 190) and "Où es-tu" (II, 193).
Just as significant, however, are the many other images, less
aggressively antitraditional, which demonstrate no less vigorously the power of love to liberate man from his depressing sense
of isolation in nature. For all Péret's poems of love lend support
to Breton's insistent claim, in the *Second Manifeste du surréalisme,* that Surrealists may be considered, historically, as "the
tail of romanticism," but, of course, *"such a prehensile tail"* (184).
Like the Romantics, Péret returns to nature, but on his own terms.

V *All or Nothing*

In his *Les Vases communicants* of 1932 André Breton asserted
that the demands of love are to be met by "abandoning ordinary
logical paths." A complementary remark occurs in the preface
to the *Anthologie de l'Amour sublime,* where Benjamin Péret
notes that one sees the object of one's love with a different eye:
"Hesitant imagination has given way to intuition, sure of itself"
(12). This is more than a reaffirmation of faith in poetry as
an intuitive apprehension of the world. For by inspiring unhesi-
tating trust in intuition, love facilitates creative liberation in a
poet about whose work Breton wrote in his *Anthologie de
l'Humour noir,* "Never have words and what they designate,
freed once and for all from domestication, manifested such
gaiety" (506). The reflective process is ruled out and poetic
intensity augmented accordingly. Then, all obstacles having
fallen away, for Benjamin Péret, as Paul Eluard wrote in his
1929 article in *Variétés,* "hope, beautiful unexpected hope, always new, the hope of love is fulfilled in the very moment it is
revealed." Through love Péret witnessed the recurrent miracle
of which Breton spoke in *Arcane 17*: "The great malediction is
raised, and it is in human love that all the regenerative power
of the world resides."

Considered in the light of these remarks by Péret's Surrealist friends, borne out in his essay "Le Noyau de la comète," prefacing the *Anthologie de l'Amour sublime,* Marie-Odile Blanquaert's reading can be seen to rest on an erroneous premise: "Péret attempts nothing less in *Feu Central* than to 'transform the world' by reinventing love" (55). To view the love poems of *Je sublime* and *Un Point c'est tout*—gathered in *Feu central*—as the fruit of an undertaking upon which their author supposedly embarked with a definite preconceived purpose constitutes a distortion of the gravest kind. It is certainly a fact that both collections, written a decade apart, depict a world transformed. However, the common bond is the presence of love that brings this transformation about, rather than an abiding wish to use love with this very end in sight. How could it be otherwise when, to Péret, love was as Breton has described it in his poem *Fata Morgana* (1940), "that promise which goes beyond our comprehension"? As the second poem of *Un Point c'est tout*, "A suivre," lets us see, Benjamin Péret experienced love as the most marvelous event in his life:

> Rien à dire de la jonquille à tête d'écureuil
> sinon que j'aime
> comme le serpent de mer aime l'heure de la sieste
> qu'il ne connaîtra jamais
>
> Nothing to say about the squirrel-headed jonquil
> if not that I'm in love
> as the sea serpent is in love with the siesta hour
> it will never know

(II, 182)

Love explains the inexplicable, inexplicably. Péret's comment in "Le Noyau de la comète" is, "When poets elevate sublime love above all other forms of love, the fantastic marvelous, withdrawing into legend, gives place to a new marvelous, which bursts forth from sublime love itself, as if to illustrate its value as an ultimate point where mind and heart come together and are allied" (62).

It is a measure of the impassioned character of Péret's comments upon love and its relationships with poetic expression that no such statement as this could have been made from a coldly theoretical standpoint. In "Le Noyau de la comète," these words stand to remind us that Benjamin Péret believed passionately that sublime love takes its origin in the individual's strongest primordial aspirations. For this reason he felt that love opens up a pathway to transformation "ending in agreement between flesh and spirit, tending to fuse them in a higher unity in which the one cannot be distinguished from the other." Desire therefore seemed to him justified so far as it brings about this fusion (20): "The marvelous and love start from a pressing human need which, in the nonreligious world, can be satisfied only at the point where the one and the other come together" (47).

The thought that circumstances of human existence offer little encouragement for holding and defending such ideas never seems to have daunted Benjamin Péret. He declared none the less in "Toute une vie" that "consubstantial with man love dissipates ceaselessly the flood of gas bent upon his destruction" (II, 242), while still acknowledging sublime love, in the *Anthologie de l'Amour sublime,* to be "a myth with demands impossible to satisfy under present world conditions" (29). The world to which he referred is the one society has created for us. Hence Péret's conviction that social man and the human being upon whose primordial aspirations he placed reliance are fundamentally antagonistic, in the measure that the development of society goes with new constraints: "Sublime love must then engage in a totally unequal fight with the society that weighs upon it. . . . Sublime love could not, in fact, admit of the least restriction: *all or nothing!*" (24). For this reason, sublime love inspires Péret to write poems that complement those we find in a unique collection he published in 1936, the same year as *Je sublime*, calling it *Je ne mange pas de ce pain-là.*

CHAPTER 9

Hate: Je ne mange pas de ce pain-là

I *A Charge of Dynamite*

IN the Batignoles Cemetery in Paris there is a granite plaque engraved:

BENJAMIN PERET
1899–1959
JE NE MANGE PAS
DE CE PAIN-LA

Around 1960, this allusion to a collection of poems with a title meaning "I'd Rather Starve" (literally "I Don't Eat That Bread"), published in 1936 in an edition of 249 copies, could easily have escaped any but the most faithful among readers of Péret's work. Only a decade or so later, after the poet's death, was *Je ne mange pas de ce pain-là* reprinted by the Association of the Friends of Benjamin Péret.

At the head of the "Notes and Variants" offered as an appendix, the Association declared they "would feel they were going against the sense of his work and the movement of his life," if they treated Péret's life and work as "objects of erudition." All the same, we find on the same page the following quasi-erudite note: "One might be surprised to see this collection, appearing in 1936, follow *Le Grand Jeu* (1928), while Benjamin Péret published in the meantime *De Derrière les fagots* (1934). The fact is that the chronology of publication in no way reflects that of composition." Why should one be surprised, except to see the authors of this text giving the impression that *Je ne mange pas de ce pain-là* ought to be detached from Péret's poetic work? Was Jean-Louis Bédouin entirely right, then, in saying, "If one reserves a place apart for a collection like *Je ne mange pas de ce pain-là,* which goes to make the finest charge of dynamite any man has ever had the audacity to put in his writings, all the other poems and collections of poems by Péret take part equally in the song of love and the cry of revolt" (71)?

Let us settle at once a couple of questions that now face us. While the tone of *Je ne mange pas* is a very special one, it is not quite without precedent in Péret's writings, as readers of the poem "S'ennuyer," in *De Derrière les fagots* (II, 66–67) can testify. Whenever Benjamin Péret had occasion to refer to priests or government ministers, or to other respected representatives of the social order, he resorted to the kind of abusive language that is so much a feature of *Je ne mange pas de ce pain-là,* for he harbored undying detestation for such people. In a number of poems he published before and after 1936 incidental details evidence comparable violence. Although scatology appears outside *Je ne mange pas* only in *Les Couilles enragées,* that erotic antireligious text, images referring to the church, the army, the police, and so on are invariably derogatory, eliciting nothing but feelings of disgust, sharpened by corrosive humor. If a poem called "Minute," that appeared in the sixth number of *Minotaure* in December, 1934, is not taken up in *Je ne mange pas de ce pain-là,* this is because it does not sustain the tone set by its reference to "the rats that are singing / mouth of drain mass and filthy lemon vespers" (I, 267). The special element lending *Je ne mange pas* its unique quality is this. The poems assembled under that arrogant title all find in violent abuse their dominant motivating energy.

Of the twenty-eight texts reprinted as *Je ne mange pas de ce pain-là* eleven were published originally between 1926 and 1929 in *La Révolution surréaliste.* Three others came out first in *Le Surréalisme au service de la Révolution* between 1930 and 1933. We are not dealing here, then, with a unified sequence of poems, conceived with a predetermined aim. In any case, setting aside the 1936 collection, as Bédouin seems to want us to do, would be an error. It is true that hate replaces love in *Je ne mange pas,* which came out the same year as *Je sublime;* but it does so only the better to raise the cry of Surrealist revolt. And, all in all, this Surrealist cry of protest is, in Péret's work, the very expression of love.

II *The Ethics of Revolt*

All the same, an attentive reader will have noticed that, while we have been able to draw freely upon a wide range of Péret poems so as to illustrate how automatism lends itself to the communication of the marvelous, no evidence at all has come from *Je ne mange pas de ce pain-là*. This volume is sufficiently distinctive in nature to be worthy of examination on its own. It brings to the presentation of the marvelous a perspective noticeably different from the one offered by the rest of Péret's poetry.

Everywhere in Péret's writing spontaneity can be seen to be a most fruitful characteristic. The poem "Toute une vie" is clearly expressive of genuine feeling and, as a sincere statement, is essential to full understanding of Péret's lifelong association with André Breton. All the same, by the standard set and attained so often elsewhere in Péret's work, "Toute une vie" is less than an impressive poetic text. The same must be said of another poem, "Violette Nozières," and of a third example of reduced poetic inspiration, Péret's longest poem, "Air mexicain."[1] The warmth of the poet's affection for Breton is not at issue. Nor is his indignation at the fate of Violette Nozières.[2] Nor again is the profound impression that Mexico and its culture made upon him. What calls for recognition, rather, is that when Benjamin Péret undertook to write occasional verse the result, on the poetic level, was generally less than satisfactory. Hence *Je ne mange pas de ce pain-là* is, by contrast, noteworthy as a brilliant exception to what other *vers de circonstance* would lead us to consider a rule, so far as his poetic practice is concerned.

More important still, of course, is the contrast to be observed between *Je ne mange pas de ce pain-là* and the poetic products of Péret's automatism. This collection offers something quite different from the rest of Péret's work, as characterized by Claude Courtot: "We have seen Breton 'envy him his remarkable lack of "composition" and that perpetual flying before the wind.' There is indeed no other guiding thread in Péret's poetry (which of course does not mean that all profound motivation is absent) than the dictation of the surreal voice to which he commits himself body and soul" (108).

What at first strikes us in *Je ne mange pas* is an air of "composition" in marked contradiction with that "perpetual flying before the wind," admired in Péret's writing by Breton.[3] One notices in a poem on the stabilization of the franc a rhythmic echo of the *Marseillaise*: "Allons enfants de la tinette / morver dans l'oreille de Poincaré" ("Let's go children of the septic tank / to rot in Poincaré's ear" [I, 260]). One can pick up a few direct quotations, like *endurance et patriotisme* for which we are indebted to Cardinal Mercier (I, 240). Also one notices elements of parody, as in a poem about the League of Nations: "Or en ce temps-là les pissotières marchant à pas cadencé / se retrouvaient à Genève" ("Now in those days pisshouses marching with rhythmic step / would find themselves in Geneva again" [I, 257]), and even more subtle allusions, likely to escape the inattentive ear. Thus two lines from "Nungesser und Coli sind Verreckt"—"mais quand ils eurent dépassé leur crachat / les requins vinrent à leur rencontre" ("but when they had passed their spittle / the sharks came to meet them" [I, 241])—are reminiscent of this subtitle which caught the Surrealists' attention during the Paris showing of a film by Murnau: "Dès que Hutter eut franchi le pont / les fantômes vinrent à sa rencontre." However, if we may suppose from indications such as these that in *Je ne mange pas* composition was less free than in *De Derrière les fagots,* for example, we must acknowledge at the same time that the image of marching urinals, like the oblique reference to Murnau's *Nosferatu, eine Symphonie des Grauens,* is entirely typical of Benjamin Péret's poetry, reflecting his viewpoint upon life without distortion.

Nevertheless Courtot omits *Je ne mange pas* altogether from his *Introduction à la lecture de Benjamin Péret.* On one level of response—that to which we have seen Courtot grant precedence —the omission is understandable, no doubt. On another, though, it is indefensible. Not a single verse from *Je ne mange pas de ce pain-là* is cited in a chapter of Courtot's book taking its title from a line in *A Tâtons*: "In a milky way of revolt." How, without mentioning *Je ne mange pas*, can one speak of revolt, as directed against the "repugnant ethics of hypocrisy, underhandedness and cowardice current in present-day society"?[4] And how can one appreciate that, for Péret, "any conservative ethics can only be the ethics of prison and of death"?[5]

III *Revulsion*

Still, it is very possible that our first impression of *Je ne mange pas de ce pain-là* may appear to be taking us away from features to which, if we are examining Péret's published collections in chronological order, his earlier writings have accustomed us. The recurrence of certain aggressively vulgar motifs can well have the effect of confronting readers with the following question: When expressing disgust in these poems of protest, was Benjamin Péret content to confine himself to a very elementary level of linguistic sophistication and imaginative activity? This question brings with it another: Would it not be right to say that here Péret was satisfied with a few fairly monotonous images, when communicating the revulsion he felt? After all, one can hardly read through *Je ne mange pas* and not notice "La mort de la mère Cognacq," which reaches its climax in these words:

> Plus de mère Cognacq
> plus d'enfants venant après dix-huit autres
> à Pâques ou à Noël
> pisser dans la marmite familiale
> Elle est crevée la mère Cognacq
> dansons dansons en rond
> sur sa tombe surmontée d'un étron

> No more Ma Cognacq
> no more children coming after eighteen others
> at Easter and Christmas
> to piss in the family cooking-pot
> she's kicked the bucket Ma Cognacq has
> Let's dance let's dance in a circle
> on her grave surmounted by a turd

(I, 251–52)

We have no hope of failing to notice that, with defecation and urination, Péret seems to take pleasure in this collection in insisting upon disgusting odors. Thus the breasts and feet of Joan of Arc, in his poem about her, have the sickening pungency of vegetables gone rotten (II, 246). Since a stench accompanies rotting, we must be prepared to see the latter accompany the former, as in this line from "6 décembre": "And Blum got up for the rotten kiss on the rotten mouth" (I, 283).

The impression communicated by verses of this kind can be misleading, however, just as much so as the occasional realistic images that find their way into Péret's short stories. To describe Joan of Arc's relations with her king (who gobbles up her feet and breasts, despite their smell), Péret does indeed use realistic elements giving, among others, this comparison indicative of his indifference to good taste, which Surrealists consider to be as confining for the creative sensibility as aesthetic theory: "Joan joins him in a street urinal / and they love one another as urine loves moist slate" (I, 246). And yet this image is by no means gratuitously shocking, since it serves to degrade people for whom Benjamin Péret felt nothing but contempt. This is to say that throughout *Je ne mange pas de ce pain-là* physical repugnance is linked with moral disgust. We see this, for example, in "Nungesser und Coli sind verreckt": "Soak old croutons in the great urinal / What salacious maniac would dare with his crumbling fingers / touch your sad rottenness" (I, 241); or again in Péret's presentation of Cardinal Mercier as "like a garbage can / overflowing with host" and "smelling of god like a stable of dung / and like dung of Jesus" (I, 239).

Whereas Arthur Rimbaud had challenged only established aesthetic values, when speaking of his Vénus Anadyomène with "broad rump / Hideously beautiful with an ulcer on the anus," Péret undermined attitudes he found unacceptable by laying a charge of humor to them. God one day appears to Cardinal Mercier "like an anus" (I, 239). "Nungesser und Coli sind verreckt" opens with the words, "Off they went / and tricolor flags came out of every anus" (I, 241). It is where bad taste and obscenity, even, join humor that the poems of *Je ne mange pas de ce pain-là* find their iconoclastic tone; in the first lines of a poem on the temporal power of the Pope, for instance:

La sueur noire des porcs
accoucha d'un pou blanc
Gras visqueux il grandit
Comme il était italian

il entreprit sa pauvre marche sur Rome
et un jour arriva au cul sale du Vatican
Ce n'était plus qu'un morpion au milieu de christs pourris
et de vierges violées par ses ancêtres

The black sweat of swine
gave birth to a white louse
Fat slimy he grew
As he was Italian
he undertook his poor march on Rome
and one day arrived at the dirty ass of the Vatican
He now was only a crab-louse among rotten christs
and virgins violated by his ancesters

(I, 243)

In similar vein are these verses from a poem about Marshal
Foch, "Vie de l'assassin Foch":

A quinze ans un âne le violait
et ça faisait un beau couple
Il en naquit une paire de bottes avec des éperons
dans laquelle il disparut comme une chaussette sale

Ce n'est rien dit le père
son bâton de maréchal est sorti de la tinette
C'est le métier qui veut cela
Le métier était beau et l'ouvrier à sa hauteur
Sur son passage des geysers de vomissements jaillissaient
et l'éclaboussaient

At fifteen he was being raped by a donkey
and a fine couple they made
From this was born a pair of boots with spurs
into which he disappeared like a dirty sock

That's nothing said the father
his marshall's baton has come from the septic tank
That goes with the job
The job was a fine one and the worker up to it
As he passed by geysers of vomit would shoot up
and spatter him

(I, 267)

IV *Beyond the* déjà-vu

If we look closely at the images in *Je ne mange pas de ce pain-là*, we find that those which impress most are not of the following kind: "We are shitty angels spat out by god / for reconciliation in France" ("6 décembre" [I, 283]), nor even comparisons in which realistic elements serve simply to set off imaginative ones: "And the noodles were wagging like the tail of a fox terrier sniffing a turd" ("La Guerre italo-abyssine" [I, 278]). More worthy of our attention are these verses borrowed from "La Peste tricolore," where Péret speaks of Chiappe, detested by Surrealists as a representative of a repressive police force:[6]

> car
> fumier professionnel
> dont le sex-appeal enivre les mouches et les égoûts
> il ne pouvait que haïr le balai qui le nettoiera

> for
> professional dung-heap
> whose sex appeal intoxicates flies and drains
> he could only hate the brush that will sweep him away
>
> (I, 276)

But above all invective finds fullest expression—as the extracts taken from "Vie de l'assassin Foch" and "Le Pouvoir temporel du Pape" suggest—when, the poem having moved outside rational limits, images develop without nostalgia for the *déjà vu*: "Long live December 6 / growled the juice from the wad of tobacco / dressed in a fleur-de-lys turd" ("6 février" [I, 280]). Opening *Je ne mange pas* to the page where Péret speaks of that curious annual display of dementia, the Tour de France cycle race, we read, "This is because France spreads out like a celestial turd / and we race around to chase off the flies" (I, 236). Moving to "Le Pacte des quatre," we come upon these lines:

> et bientôt on ne vit plus qu'un petit tas de généraux
> auréolés de mouches
> qui tournoyaient autour des quatre drapeaux
> plantés dans leurs fesses

and soon all that could be seen was a small heap of generals
haloed by flies
flying in circles about the four flags
planted in their buttocks

(I, 254)

As for the poem about Joan of Arc, in conversation with
"cow-dung haloed by flies / neighbor to an old piece of rotten
wood / that toads get their exercise from jumping over," its
heroine shows no hesitation in interpreting the words she hears:

Alors Jeanne comprit qu'elle était en face de Dieu
et avala la bouse comme une relique
Aussitôt Dieu se cristallisa sous forme d'hémorroïdes
et tous les chiens de Domrémy lui léchèrent le derrière

Then Joan understood that she was before God
and swallowed the cow dung like a relic
At once God crystallized in the form of hemorrhoids
and all the dogs in Domrémy licked her backside

(I, 245)

In their turn, images in which rottenness and putrefaction
figure display the same tendency to overflow the real. Péret
borrows realistic ingredients here only to support comparisons
in which familiar reality is flouted. The generals in "Nungesser
und Coli sind verreckt" appear before us "covered in vomit"
(I, 242). As for the Jesuits in a poem about the decline of the
franc, "their eucharistic rottenness fills every chalice" (I, 258).
"Jeanne d'Arc" depicts "fourteen archbishops with putrescible
glances" (I, 246), and "6 février" refers to "Rotten yellow green
curés," fondling adolescent buttocks (I, 280). Celebrating the
passing of a politician, Briand, Péret writes:

Maintenant qu'il est crevé nous pouvons dire
qu'il était notre frère comme le porc et le rat pesteux
Comme nous il sa vautrait dans l'ordure et le fumier
et maintenant qu'il est crevé
nous lui rendons cette ordure avec notre bénédiction
Seigneur bénissez-nous avec le balai des cabinets
comme nous l'avons béni avec du poisson pourri

> Now that he's kicked the bucket we can say
> that he was our brother like the pig and the plaguy rat
> Like us he wallowed in garbage and dung
> and now that he's kicked the bucket
> we return this garbage to him with our blessing
> Lord bless us with the toilet-bowl brush
> as we have blessed him with rotten fish

(I, 262)

On the subject of Chiappe, "La Peste tricolore" assures us:

> Plus tard
> plus rabougri encore
> il fermenta longuement
> dans la fosse où l'on fait des flics
> qui deviendront un si beau jeu de massacre

> Later on
> even more stunted
> he fermented a long time
> in the cess-pit in which cops are made
> that will become such fine Aunt Sallies

(I, 276)

And in a passage where subordinate clauses follow a characteristic antirational development, "Louis XVI s'en va à la guillotine" depicts the king's execution in these terms:

> Il pleut du sang de la neige
> et toutes sortes de saletés
> qui jaillissent de sa vieille carcasse
> de chien crevé au fond d'une lessiveuse
> au milieu du linge sale
> qui a eu le temps de pourrir
> comme la fleur de lis des poubelles
> que les vaches refusent de brouter
> parce qu'elle répand une odeur de dieu
> dieu le père des boues
> qui a donné à Louis XVI
> le droit divin de crever
> comme un chien dans une lessiveuse

It is raining blood snow
and all sorts of filth
that bursts from his old
dead dog's carcass in a washing machine
among dirty linen
that has had time to rot
like the fleur-de-lis of garbage cans
that cows refuse to graze
because it gives off a smell of god
god the father of mud
who gave Louis XVI
the divine right to kick the bucket
like a dog in a washing machine

(I, 238)

Looking next at olfactive images, we find in "Peau de tigre" lines that bring to mind Péret's reference to the "pestilential miasmas of religion" in his *Anthologie des Mythes*:

Vieil animal oublié dans une cave
rien ne lui manquait
pas même l'haleine fétide des résidus de goupillon
et des habitués de caserne

An old animal forgotten in a cellar
he lacked nothing
not even the fetid breath of aspergillum refuse
and of habitual visitors to army barracks[7]

(I, 264)

In "La baisse du franc" we hear of "skeletal billy-goats / that spread all around their Gallic Christian stink" (I, 258). Then in "La loi Paul Boncour" Péret shows that a Rabelaisian echo can make a useful contribution where invective exceeds the bounds of reasonableness: "And somewhere the firing line will be guarded by polecats / the smell of which carried by a favorable wind / will suffocate whole regiments / better than an episcopal fart" (I, 255–56).

The more violent Péret becomes, the more his images advance beyond the boundaries set up by realist convention. "Vie de l'assassin Foch" begins as follows:

Un jour d'une mare de purin une bulle monta
et creva
A l'odeur le père reconnut
Ce sera un fameux assassin

One day from a pool of liquid manure a bubble rose
and burst
At the smell the father acknowledged
He'll be a great killer

(I, 267)

Farther on, Péret speaks of the "bilious puke of the military medal" and the "nauseating hog-wash of the legion of honor / that grew little by little" (I, 268). In "La Peste tricolore" Chiappe, "an old wad of tobacco sucked and sucked again," is described as "Born of vomit in a blue chamber pot" (I, 276). And in "6 décembre" Péret stresses "the odor of old guts" hanging over the Chamber of Deputies where, incidentally, the seats are "crawling with maggots" (I, 282). Here, in the scene he depicts, as everywhere else, Péret demonstrates his complete disregard for rational preconceptions:

Soudain un mou de veau auréolé de mouches
suant des patriotismes
comme un général devant le monument de ses morts
un mou de veau se leva
et le président grogna
M. Ybarnégaray peut vomir
On vit alors s'échappant du cancer de sa langue
voltiger les bananes pourries qu'écrasaient les
                              oranges sures de ses yeux
Et les rinçures du pavillon de la boucherie
qui débordaient de ce fétide évier
réjouissaient les narines des assistants dont on ferait
                              un si bon engrais
et qui sentaient dans leur nombril crasseux
en forme de tête de mort molle
germer la pomme de terre gelée d'un drapeau tricolore

Suddenly a calf's lung haloed by flies
sweating patriotisms

like a general before the monument to his dead
a calf's lung stood up
and the president growled
Mr Ybarnégaray may vomit
Then could be seen given off by the cancer of his tongue
the rotten bananas flitting past crushed by the sour
                                              oranges of his eyes
And the slops from the butchers' shed
that overflowed from this fetid sink
delighted the nostrils of the spectators from whom
                         such good manure could be made
and who felt in their filthy navels
shaped like a soft death's head
the frozen potato of a tricolor flag germinating

                                                    (I, 282–83)

V Reconnaissance

In these last lines the function of descriptive detail is entirely
in accord with that usually reserved for them in Péret's writing.
The navels we are shown are not only filthy but shaped like a
death's head. And the latter, which we would not have expected
to see invoked in relation to navels is—even more unlikely—a soft
one. Each qualifying detail submits a familiar object, or even a
less than familiar one, to unforeseen modification. Each goes a
step farther than the one before in a direction where habitual
reality clearly does not lie: the more we learn about the navels
in the public gallery of the Chamber of Deputies, the less they
resemble our own. And there is good reason for this, we discover
when we turn to *La Parole est à Péret*: "for the barbarous society
that makes the vast majority of men live (live?) in cans and
preserves them in cans, quarters with the dimensions of a coffin,
putting a price on the sun and the sea, tries to bring them back
intellectually, also, to an immemorial period, prior to the reconnaissance of poetry" (26–27).
It may seem ridiculous to try to illustrate with the example
of a soft death's head navel Péret's concept of poetry as reconnaissance, especially when, in the French word *reconnaissance*,
the idea of searching is intimately caught up with recognition—
knowing again something that society has attempted to make us

forget. And yet if we disregard this example, chosen at random from among many, we come close to falsifying perspectives, as we ask ourselves what part is played by the marvelous in poems where hate apparently predominates.

We know well enough that *La Parole est à Péret* called for total nonconformity on the part of a poet who wishes to fulfill his revolutionary role. However, anyone who concludes that Benjamin Péret proved to be a poet in *Je ne mange pas de ce pain-là* because he revealed in these poems that he detested priests, politicians, and army officers sees his work out of focus. In Péret's writing, opposition is not poetic because it rests on moral indignation; it is both poetic and expressive of an ethical position at the same time. Benjamin Péret's response to the question, "Why don't you believe in God?" was categorical: "The idea of such a sinister ghost is already an offense to humanity. Let those who believe in it first demonstrate its existence to us. It's not up to me to prove I haven't murdered my concierge."[8] We are back to that objection, voiced in *La Parole est à Péret*, directed against the idea of deity which slips the straitjacket of religious dogmas on poetry. An article written by Péret not long before his death evidences the continuity of his thought on the subject. Describing the poor quarter of Manaus on January 18, 1956, Péret commented, "Everywhere, open doors and windows make visible in the shadows the vile Christian symbol for which the sole purpose, here, is to stifle all revolt at birth so that misery may seem a gift from heaven."[9] It is small wonder that Péret consistently treated God as "an obstacle to all knowledge," to cite *La Parole est à Péret*, when religion seemed to him destined to stifle all revolt.

Nowhere in quite the same way as in *Je ne mange pas de ce pain-là* does the marvelous function in Péret's writings "like a time-bomb" ready to explode. Nowhere does it "grab you by the throat" with quite the same grip. Speaking of the riots of February 6, 1934, Péret exclaimed, "How fine it was / The buses burned like the heretics of old." Meanwhile, he tells us, horses' eyes struck "cops so repugnant and so greasy / that you'd have taken them for crosses of fire" (I, 280). Talking of the "Congrès eucharistique de Chicago" meant to Péret recalling that "Judas sold god like French fries / and his bones have

scratched the hooves of purebred horses" (I, 249). All it takes
to describe Cardinal Mercier are these two lines: "an asthmatic /
dressed in red like a flayed calf" (I, 240). And André Gide's
conversion to Communism inspires these verses:

> Tel une tomate agitée par le vent
> Monsieur le camarade Gide fait un foutu drapeau rouge
> dont aucune salade ne voudrait
>
> Like a tomato shaken by the wind
> Comrade Gide looks a hell of a red flag
> that no salad would touch

                                                      (I, 244)

And with reason; for this flag, according to Péret, "hides a
cross / dipped in vitriol." How else should one speak of the
death in 1932 of Aristide Briand, eleven times President of the
Council, than in the following terms:

> Enfin ce sperme mal bouilli jaillit du bordel maternel
> un rameau d'olivier dans le cul
> Terrine d'eaux grasses
> coiffant le chou-fleur socialiste
> qui se frottait les fesses
> sur le drapeau français
> en pétant
> La France est le roi des animaux
> le pays des capotes anglaises
> Vive la France
> et les chiens décorés
> du sang de 1 500 000 morts
> qui enrichirent des ventres ballonnés
> Voilà Monsieur Briand
>
> At last this half-boiled sperm burst forth from the maternal brothel
> an olive branch up its ass
> A pot of greasy water
> on the head of the socialist cauliflower
> that wiped its buttocks
> on the French flag
> farting

France is king of the animals
the land of French letters[10]
Long live France
and dogs decorated
with the blood of 1,500,000 dead
who added to swollen bellies
That's Mr Briand

(I, 261)

"Le Tour de France cycliste" begins, "Whether our ears
are Chinese lanterns or dead fish we race." In Péret's universe,
Chinese lanterns and dead fish vie with one another for the
role of ears. So nothing can stand between the poet and the
right to proceed to tell his readers:

Mais voici que dieu a craché sur la route
et traînant sa sottise comme un parapluie
a tracé des ornières jonchées de crucifix
Malheur au coureur imprudent qui s'y engage comme
            un cheval sous un tunnel
Jésus sort de sa croix et plante son cœur dans les
            boyaux de la bécane

But now god has spat on the road
and dragging his stupidity behind him like an umbrella
has traced ruts strewn with crucifixes
Woe betide the imprudent racer who gets into those
            like a horse in a tunnel
Jesus comes down from his cross and plants his heart
            in the bike's tubular tires

(I, 237)

The same kind of effect is achieved in "Nungesser und Coli sind
verreckt," where the marvelous takes command, thanks to the
movement of the poem from everyday experience into the world
of imagination:

Dans l'égout du ciel français
ils étaient à leur aise mieux que des crapauds
mais quand ils eurent dépassé leur crachat
les requins vinrent à leur rencontre

les rejoignirent quelque part entre deux vagues
surmontés d'un chapeau haut-de-forme
comme des croque-morts patriotiques
Mais ils étaient déjà pourris
et dans leurs yeux les vers simulaient des points d'interrogation
Les vagues crachèrent de dégoût à leur approche
et dans un hoquet les avalèrent

In the drain of the French sky
they were more at ease than toads
but when they had passed their spittle
the sharks came to meet them
joined them somewhere between two waves
surmounted by a top hat
like patriotic undertaker's men
But they were already rotten
and in their eyes worms feigned to be question marks
The waves spat with disgust at their approach
and in one hiccup swallowed them

(I, 241)

Everywhere comparisons that are quite irrational, or are incongruously realistic in the context of a Péret poem, ("like patriotic undertaker's men") and in which *like* defies the reasonable world, help disorient us and redirect thought and feeling from habitual paths. Péret remained throughout his life master of the unassimilable comparison, ever elusive of domestication. The poet who did not hesitate to refer upon occasion to the emblematic turd never ceased to demonstrate that he would rather starve than swallow the bread consecrated by society. To those who might have been less on their guard than he, more inclined to accept without question the diet prescribed by social living, Benjamin Péret offered *Je ne mange pas de ce pain-là,* where the marvelous is an emetic.

CHAPTER 10

Conclusion

I *"The Lucid Glance of a Glove Shop"*[1]

IN the final analysis, André Breton once argued in the name of Surrealism, everything depends upon our power of "voluntary hallucination." Breton's phrase is one that must provoke reflection in anyone truly interested in the poetic aspirations that Surrealists have attempted to define and, more important still, to attain. Is the adjective he used really compatible with the noun it qualifies? Or do we face a contradiction in terms, grave enough to cast doubt upon the seriousness of Surrealist poetic endeavor? Are we, indeed, obliged to dismiss Surrealism, in the end, as a self-defeating program, inextricably entangled in paradox, or perhaps a hoax practiced for half a century, at the public's expense?

Nothing is to be gained, we can be sure, by turning to Benjamin Péret in the hope of receiving a formal response to any of these questions and related ones. No Surrealist more consistently than he showed so little inclination to reason with his audience, on their ground and in terms of their choosing. All the same, one thing is clear, both in Péret's published declarations on the subject of poetry and in the poetic texts he has left behind. As the direct consequence of voluntary choice, his work represents his persistent willingness to accept a calculated risk. At all times Péret gave precedence to hallucinated and hallucinating visions, liberated in creative consciousness by the uncensored flow of imaginative inspiration, with which he never ceased to identify authentic poetic expression.

The voluntary element in Péret's writing is more appropriately defined, therefore, if we first seek our bearings by examining, to begin with, which notions of creative effort the poet

155

156 BENJAMIN PÉRET

categorically rejects—from the pursuit of formal perfection to the expression of political conviction—rather than if we ask what he was trying to grasp through poetry. In Péret's case, certainly, Surealism found its generative energy in a freedom from convention and custom which, far from controlling hallucination in some deliberate way, solicited its uninhibited manifestation. In fact, Péret's distinction as a Surrealist poet owes very much indeed to the way—deceptively easy in appearance —he was able to achieve that freedom and turn it to account.

The work of some of the best-known Surrealist poets is characterized by a gravity typified in the poems of Breton, or René Char, or Gui Rosey. Péret impresses by qualities of a totally different nature. And yet these have nothing to do with the celebrated "facility" of Eluard's verse. This is why, viewed from within the Surrealist movement, Péret appears as Naville described him in *La Revue européenne*, not only "the king of imagination," but also a poet "scandalous in essence," possessed of "a great apocalyptic verve on which we really must become intoxicated." If his writings seem to some to rest upon a paradox, this impression survives longest in the minds of those who share the position of Michel Carrouges, never a surrealist, incidentally. Writing in *Preuves* in December of the year Péret died, Carrouges affirmed, apropos of Péret's poetry, "It is possible that we lose our footing a thousand times, trying to follow it, but by the very fact that it appears incomprehensible, it expresses what man is as an indomitable spirit of negation."

One can speak of Benjamin Péret's work as incomprehensible only at the cost of asserting a fatal inconsistency between his theory and his practice as a poet. In 1950 Péret confirmed that he believed profoundly in the communicability of poetic vision through poetic expression, when he firmly condemned in his essay "La Soupe déshydratée" the idea that each individual writer speaks only to himself, in the "language of a deaf man" (51). True, his own writings initially present most readers with some difficulty, as though he were indeed speaking a private language. This is because Péret remained throughout his adult life faithful to the principle of automatism. He neither would nor could reach out reassuringly to invite reluctant visitors into his poetic domain, facilitating their passage from familiar reality into poetic reality. But in accusing Benjamin Péret of being incomprehensible, we succeed only in confessing to our own inadequacies.

Bailly comes closer to essentials than Carrouges, when he observes, "Saying yes to everything that surfaces as words go by, the surrealist poet says no to this world, and his logos is only the tension between a world that is and a world that is not, but can be" (70). Important for real appreciation of Péret's work as a poet, and of his stature among Surrealists, is recognition of the significant fact that the tension to which Bailly perceptively refers is higher, and hence more noticeable upon first contact with his work, than it is with any other Surrealist poet. And this is so for the very good reason that Benjamin Péret's devotion to exploring the *other* world of the marvelous was unencumbered by any vestige of respect for habitual reality.

It is not surprising that most people whom Péret's poetry leaves bemused or annoyed have a tendency to foist responsibility for their dissatisfaction upon the author of these supposedly impertinent texts. This is and will always be their privilege. All the same, it is important to notice that, while Eluard's facility is generally considered enviable and Péret's creative verve is identified far less widely with true poetic accomplishment, Paul Eluard once confessed, "Péret is a greater poet than I."[2]

In its phenomenal richness, Benjamin Péret's work epitomizes some of the central ambitions of Surrealism, typified in some of the most characteristic features of the Surrealists' poetic program. Love, humor, imagination, invective, all find expression through his writings with special acuity, so that if future generations were to have access to the work of no other Surrealist than he, they would have to hand evidence reliable enough for them to form an accurate impression of the major themes of Surrealist poetry. And indeed, ever since the inception of Surrealist activity none of these themes, as Surrealists have used them, could have been defined adequately without reference to their development in Péret's work.

Benjamin Péret represents Surrealism as no other writer has done. But this does not mean that his work is to be considered valuable only for the fidelity with which it mirrors Surrealist aspirations and the ways they have been pursued. His work remains uniquely his own, his originality unquestionable and inimitable in its spontaneity. For in Péret's writings irrationality is an effect, not an aim provocatively pursued at the risk of alienating the public. Irrationality points to the ever-renewed triumph of the pleasure principle through a rectification of reality that, in Péret's opinion, it is the natural function of poetry to attain and the role of the marvelous to communicate.

Notes and References

Unless otherwise indicated, the place of publication for all books is Paris.

Chapter One

1. See Jean-Marie Mabire, "Entretiens avec Philippe Soupault," *Etudes cinématographiques* 38–39 (1965), 31.

2. Eric Sellin, review of J. H. Matthews, *Surrealist Poetry in France, Books Abroad* (October, 1970). Marcel Fourrier has commented on Péret (*Libération*, September 29, 1959), "His contempt for literature carries him onto ground where cowards, conformists, pedants have not dared follow him."

3. Henri Peyre, review of Matthews, *Surrealist Poetry in France, Symposium* (Winter, 1970).

4. André Breton, *Entretiens 1913–1952* (Gallimard, 1952), p. 68, calls Péret "celui qui s'est jetè sans freins dans l'aventure poétique."

5. José Pierre, *Le Surréalisme: dictionnaire de poche* (Fernand Hazan, éditeur, 1973), p. 135 (English edition distributed in England by Eyre Methuen). It is true that certain of Péret's poems offer variants which suggest that he had second thoughts now and again. This does not alter the fact that Benjamin Péret found in automatism the guiding principle of his writing: none of the variants, it should be noted, evidences any adjustment of the poetic statement to the demands of reasonable discourse.

6. André Breton, *Nadja* [1928] (Gallimard, 1949), pp. 34–35. Richard Howard's version of this passage in his translation of *Nadja* (New York: Grove Press, 1960), p. 28, is ungrammatical as well as inaccurate.

7. Péret rejected Dada early. See his essay "A travers mes yeux," *Littérature*, n.s., no. 5 (October, 1922), p. 13. Cf. his article "Des Eaux usées," *BIEF: Jonction surréaliste*, no. 2 (December 15, 1958). Péret's disagreement with the promoter of Dada in France, Tristan Tzara, led to a confrontation on the occasion of Tzara's 1948 lecture at the Sorbonne, published the same year by Nagel as *Le Surréalisme et l'après-guerre*. See too Péret's attack on both Tzara and Aragon, "Paillasse et son roquet chéri," *Médium: Communication surréaliste*, n.s., no. 2 (February, 1954), 11.

8. Victor Crastre, *Le Drame du surréalisme* (Les Editions du temps, 1963), p. 68.

9. Jehan Mayoux, "Benjamin Péret, la fourchette coupante," *Le Surréalisme, même,* no. 2 (Spring, 1957), 152. This is the first part of an essay continued in the third issue of the same magazine (Autumn, 1957), where the photo of Péret insulting a priest is reproduced p. 57.

Claude Courtot has given interesting development to Mayoux's thesis on the complementary roles of Breton and Péret. See his *Introduction à la lecture de Benjamin Péret* (Le Terrain Vague, 1965), pp. 75–95.

10. Péret expanded *La Parole est à Péret,* adding several pages at the end, before his volume finally appeared as *Anthologie des Mythes, légendes et contes populaires d'Amérique* (Editions Albin Michel, 1960).

11. While Péret believed Trotsky's name to be so intimately associated with ideas of social emancipation in our time that it is impossible to speak of revolution without speaking of Trotsky, he was no blind disciple. See the criticisms set forth in his article on Trotsky, "Sa Vie," *Médium: Communication surréaliste,* n.s., no. 3 (May, 1954), 32–36.

12. Courtot (*Introduction,* pp. 26–27) reproduces eight letters written by Péret to Breton from Spain during 1936 and 1937. For an evaluation of Péret's role in Spain see the letter from Juan Andrade to the editor of *Arts* (December 6, 1962), reproduced in a collective posthumous tribute called *De la part de Péret,* published without name of publisher or date, in 1962 (p. 11).

13. Published under the auspices of a group called Fomento Obrero Revolucionario; *Pour un Second Manifeste Communiste* appeared in bilingual text, French and Spanish (Le Terrain Vague, 1965).

14. Political writings by Péret and Munis were collected as an attack upon the trade unions, *Les Syndicats contre la révolution* (Le Terrain Vague, 1968), with a preface by Jehan Mayoux. Péret's contribution took the form of a series of articles originally published in the newspaper *Le Libertaire*—organ of the Anarchist Federation—on June 26, July 10, July 24, August 7, August 21, and September 4, 1952.

15. *Le Déshonneur des poètes* précéde de *La Parole est à Péret* (J. J. Pauvert, 1965), pp. 16–17. *Le Déshonneur des poètes* appeared originally in Mexico City, under the imprint Poésie et Révolution. Page references below are to the Pauvert edition.

16. Franklin Rosemont, "An Introduction to Benjamin Péret," *Radical America* 4, no. 6 (August, 1970), 11.

17. Jean-Louis Bédouin, "Introduction," *Benjamin Péret* (Seghers, 1961), p. 57.

18. "Anyway, I recall: it was in Rennes Prison that *they* had shut me up in the month of May, 1940, because I'd committed the crime of considering that such a society was my enemy, if only for having obliged me, like so many others, to defend it twice in my lifetime when I admitted to having nothing in common with it" (Pauvert edition, p. 38).

19. Responding to an "Inquiry among European writers into the spirit of America," conducted by the magazine *transition*, in answer to the question, "How, in your opinion, are the influences of the United States manifesting themselves upon Europe, and in Europe?" Péret wrote, "Through the most emphatic garbage, the ignoble sense of money, the indigence of ideas, the savagery of hypocrisy in morals, and altogether through a loathsome swinishness pushed to the point of paroxysm." *transition* 13 (Summer, 1928), 250.

20. Both letters are reproduced in Courtot, *Introduction*.

21. Letter of Dec. 10, 1973, to the author from the painter Manina.

22. André Breton, *Anthologie de l'Humour noir* [1940], revised edition (J. J. Pauvert, 1966), p. 507.

Chapter Two

1. Jean-Christophe Bailly, *Au-delà du langage: une étude de Benjamin Péret* (Eric Losfeld, 1971), p. 5.

2. Georges-Emmanuel Clancier, *Panorama critique de Rimbaud au surréalisme* (Seghers, 1955), p. 463.

3. Pierre Naville, "Benjamin Péret," *La Revue européenne*, no. 26, April 1, 1925.

4. Mary Ann Caws, *The Poetry of Dada and Surrealism* (Princeton: Princeton University Press, 1970), p. 14.

5. This article appeared subsequently as "Thought is ONE and indivisible" in the English Surrealist magazine *Free Unions libres* (1946), 3–4. In Simon Watson Taylor's translation, the sentence, "La poésie est ailleurs, maniant fébrilement l'indispensable guillotine," is ludicrously rendered as "Poverty is elsewhere, wielding the indispensable guillotine feverishly." In addition, one or two phrases from the original text are omitted.

6. It is difficult to follow Elizabeth Jackson Hanchett when she claims that this definition of the unconscious is actually Péret's way of defining "universal Jungian imagination" ("The Cosmic Interpre-

tation of Benjamin Péret: A Reading of 'Une île dans une tasse'," *Dada/Surrealism* [1972], p. 42). Nowhere in the writings of Péret is Jung mentioned.

7. Louis Aragon, *La Peinture au défi*, catalog of an exhibition of collages, held in Paris at the Galerie Goemans in 1929–1930. The catalog was published in 1930 and is reprinted in Aragon, *Les Collages* (Hermann, 1965), pp. 35–71.

8. *Histoire naturelle* (Ussel: privately printed, 1958).

9. *Mort aux Vaches et au champ d'honneur* was written in the winter of 1922–1923. It appeared for the first time in 1953 under the imprint Editions Arcanes and was reprinted by Eric Losfeld in 1967. Page references below are to the latter edition.

10. *Le Gigot, sa vie et son œuvre* (Le Terrain Vague, 1957). A shorter selection of Péret's stories appeared earlier as *Main forte* (Editions K, 1947).

11. *La Brebis galante*, originally published by Les Editions premières in 1949, was reprinted by Le Terrain Vague in 1959. Its title plays upon the phrase "brebis galeux," meaning a scabby sheep, or the black sheep of the family. Page references below are to the Terrain Vague edition.

Chapter Three

1. The commentary written by Péret for the Surrealist documentary *L'Invention du monde*, filmed by Jean-Louis Bédouin and Michel Zimbacca in 1952, is evidence enough of the antiscientific source of his poetry. For further details see J. H. Matthews, *Surrealism and Film* (Ann Arbor: University of Michigan Press, 1971), pp. 116–19.

2. The phrase borrowed by Péret occurs in the first Surrealist manifesto. See André Breton, *Les Manifestes du surréalisme* (J. J. Pauvert, n.d. [1962]), p. 48.

Chapter Four

1. Jean-Louis Bédouin reports (25) that Benjamin Péret once confessed to having begun by writing poems inspired by Mallarmé—an initiation into poetry that would explain his mother's allusion, cited in Breton's *Nadja*, to someone "who'd like to get started in literature." A note at the end of the second volume of Péret's *Œuvres complètes* reproduces an untitled poem, originally published in *Les Tablettes littéraires et artistiques* on February 15, 1919. Without hesitation, the volume editors interpret this text as a "hoax." They suggest that

Péret may even have reproduced textually a little-known text by an unidentified Symbolist poet, or again that "Je rêve de musique indolente, et fanée . . ." is a pastiche, undertaken simply for its author's amusement. At all events, a comparable poem, "Importé du Japon," first published in *Action*, no. 4 (July, 1920), treats the language of Symbolism merely as a contrastive element, to set off violent imagery that will be typical of Péret's maturity as a poet.

Two unpublished stories I have had the opportunity to examine, thanks to the courtesy of Jehan Mayoux—"Sur la route de la fortune" and "Le Nègre et la soucoupe enflammée," both probably dating from the very early twenties—could have found their way into *Le Gigot, sa vie et son œuvre* without in the least looking out of place.

2. This title plays upon the homonyms *"seins"* and *"saints"*: ". . . And the Breasts were dying. . . ."

3. Published in *Le Surréalisme, même*, no. 5 (Spring, 1959), 42–44.

4. Benjamin Péret, "Le Pensée au-dessus de tout" ("Poetry above all else"), *BIEF: Jonction surréaliste* no. 1 (November 15, 1958), p. 1.

5. Marko Ristic, a response under the title "Humor in 1932" to a survey opened in the first number of *Nadrealizam danas i ovde* [Surrealism Here and Now] (June 1931), on the theme "Is Humor a Moral Attitude?" Ristic's response appeared in the second number of the same magazine (January, 1932). Under the title "L'Humour, attitude morale?" and over the signature "Marco Ristitch," it is reproduced in French translation in the sixth issue of the Parisian magazine *Le Surréalisme au service de la Révolution* (May, 1933), 36–39, and not, as reported by Yves Duplessis (*Le Surréalisme* [Presses Universitaires de France, 1950], p. 21), in *La Révolution surréaliste*.

6. Paul Eluard, "L'Arbitraire, la contradiction, la violence, la poésie," *Variétés*, June 15, 1929.

7. André Breton, "Signe ascendant" (December 30, 1947), reprinted in his *La Clé des champs* (Les Editions du Sagittaire, 1953), pp. 112–15.

8. André Breton, *L'Amour fou* [1937] (Gallimard, 1957), p. 61.

9. Nicolas Calas, "Towards a Third Surrealist Manifesto," *New Directions in Prose and Poetry*, 1940.

10. I trust that, in disagreeing with Mary Ann Caws, I am not distorting her statement, "A child's imagination and curiosity are all that is needed." "Péret—Plausible Surrealist," *Yale French Studies*, no. 31 (May, 1964), 10.

11. Benjamin Péret, "Wifredo Lam," *Médium: Communication surréaliste*, n.s., no. 4 (January, 1955), 1.

12. André Breton, "Le Merveilleux contre le mystère," *Minotaure*, no. 9 (October 15, 1936), reprinted in his *La Clé des champs*, pp. 7–12. This is the text in which Breton speaks of "pure and simple abandon to the *marvelous*" as "the source of eternal communication between men" (12).

13. Robert Benayoun's phrase is taken from a statement he made during the BBC's "Third Programme" discussion "In Defence of Surrealism," broadcast in February, 1960. The Surrealist Benayoun is the compiler of an *Anthologie du Nonsense* published by J. J. Pauvert in 1959.

14. Pierre Prigioni has made an interesting attempt at a structuralist analysis of one of Péret's tales, "Au 125 du boulevard Saint-Germain." See his "Contes populaire et conte surréaliste (approche structuraliste d'un conte de Benjamin Péret)," in *Differenze* 9 (1970), 203–23.

Chapter Five

1. The generally accepted viewpoint upon poetry is most often the one that underlies Bernard Weinberg's *The Limits of Symbolism: Studies of Five Modern French Poets* (Chicago and London: The University of Chicago Press, 1966). It rests in part upon the assumption that "an art of poetry does exist": "But we know that as a poet composes, he constantly makes choices; where to begin his poem, how to continue it, where to end it; the object or the word or the figure to be introduced at each point; the sounds and the rhythms to be developed; the emotions to be aroused and directed. These choices result from his art. . . . In each case, the choice depends upon a conception or an instinct relative to the form that the whole will ultimately take, and the 'art' consists in determining, at every point, which of the alternative solutions is to be adopted" (1). Needless to say, no Surrealist figures among Weinberg's modern poets. When Péret's work is viewed in the light of Weinberg's statement of faith, in fact, he assumes the status of supremely antiartistic poet—the very status to which he aspired.

2. Paul Eluard, *Donner à voir* (Gallimard, 1939), p. 147.

3. Quotations from Péret's poems are identified by the name of the collection from which they are taken. The original publication date for the collection in question is given upon first citation only. All references are to Benjamin Péret, *Œuvres complètes* (Eric Losfeld), volume I (1969) and volume II (1971).

4. Benjamin Péret, *Anthologie de l'Amour sublime* (Albin Michel, 1956), p. 57.

5. Readers who find these lines hard to assimilate may wish to try their luck with *taupe* in its other senses: "prostitute" or "wen."

6. Benjamin Péret, "La Soupe déshydratée," dated August, 1949, *La Nef*, no. 63–64 (March–April, 1950), "Almanach surréaliste du demi-siècle," 54.

Chapter Six

1. Raymond Roussel, *Comment j'ai écrit certains de mes livres* [1935] (J. J. Pauvert, 1963), pp. 13–14.

2. For a fuller discussion of Roussel's technique, in English, see J. H. Matthews, *Surrealism and the Novel* (Ann Arbor: University of Michigan Press, 1966), pp. 41–55.

3. In this connection, the essay "Inspiration to Order," in Max Ernst's *Beyond Painting* (New York: Wittenborn, Schultze, 1948), pp. 20–25, is of central importance.

4. André Breton, preface to his *Le Revolver à Cheveux blancs* (Editions des Cahiers libres, 1932).

5. A line from Péret's 1949 poem dedicated to André Breton, "Toute une vie," runs, "L'écriture automatique allait multiplier les merveilles que l'œil ouvert dissipait."

6. Naville's article from *La Revue européene* is reproduced in Benjamin Péret, *Œuvres complètes*, vol. II.

7. Ferdinand Alquié, *La Philosophie du surréalisme* (Flammarion, 1955), p. 155.

8. In Bernard Waldrop's translation of Alquié's volume, *The Philosophy of Surrealism* (Ann Arbor: University of Michigan Press, 1965), the word "*évidentes*" is mistranslated as "obvious."

9. The complete text appears in Paul Eluard, *Le Poète et son ombre*, ed. Paul Valette (Seghers, 1963), p. 107.

10. André Breton, introduction, dated 1949, to Jean Ferry, *Le Mécanicien et autres contes* (Par les soins les Cinéastes bibliophiles, 1950), reissued by Gallimard in 1953. Breton's prefatory essay is reprinted in his *La Clé des champs*, pp. 213–23. The passage quoted here occurs on p. 220.

11. Breton returns in his *Arcane 17* (1944) to attack the opinions and interdicts that maintain "opacity" in man.

12. André Breton, *Les Vases communicants* [1932] (Gallimard, 1955), p. 148.

Chapter Seven

1. Benjamin Péret, "A garder précieusement," a poem first published in the sixth number of the Surrealist magazine *Néon*.

2. Lautréamont's influence upon the Breton-Soupault play is discussed in J. H. Matthews, *Theatre in Dada and Surrealism* (Syracuse, N.Y.: Syracuse University Press, 1974), pp. 98–108.

3. Max Ernst, "Inspiration to Order," in his *Beyond Painting*, p. 21.

4. Max Ernst, "Beyond Painting," in his *Beyond Painting*, p. 12.

5. André Breton, "Les Mots sans rides," in his *Les Pas perdus* [1924] (Gallimard, 1949), p. 171.

6. Benjamin Péret, "Toute une vie" (July 15–23, 1949), first published in André Breton: *Essais et témoignages*, ed., Marc. Eideldinger (Neuchatel: à la Baconnière, 1950).

Chapter Eight

1. Benjamin Péret, *Anthologie de l'Amour sublime*, p. 70.

2. The eleven poems of *Un Point c'est tout* appeared for the first time in the Parisian magazine *Les 4 Vents*, no. 4 ("L'Evidence surréaliste"), 1946. They were reprinted under the same title in Péret's *Feu central* (Editions K., 1947).

3. Mary Ann Caws has sought to differentiate Péret's idea of love from Breton's. See her article "The 'Amour sublime' of Benjamin Péret: Just another 'Amour fou'?" *The French Review* 11, no. 2 (November, 1966), taken up in the chapter on Péret in her *The Inner Theatre of Recent French Poetry* (Princeton: Princeton University Press, 1972), pp. 75–105. Courtot also draws a distinction between the two (pp. 87–88). But neither he nor Mrs. Caws claims that any fundamental disagreement existed between Péret and Breton.

4. This is a biographical detail, not widely known, to which Péret refers in an essay attacking an article by the former Surrealist Georges Sadoul, in the commemorative issue of the magazine *Europe* dedicated to Eluard. See Benjamin Péret, "Défense de mentir," *Médium: Communication suréaliste*, n.s., no. 1 (November, 1953), 5–6.

5. In 1959, Aragon's text, its title delicately trimmed to *Irene*, appeared over the name of Albert de Routisie in a translation by Lowell Blair, published by Grove Press in New York.

6. *Les Couilles enragées* (Enraged Balls) first appeared under the pseudonym of Satyremont, in 1954. The publisher, Eric Losfeld, had the book bound under a false cover bearing the title *Les Rouilles encagées* (Encaged Rust). This precaution did not protect the volume from the vigilance of the French police, who in 1974 were to succeed finally in driving Losfeld, director of the publishing house Le Terrain Vague, out of business. *Les Couilles enragées* was promptly con-

fiscated. Benjamin Péret was not identified as its author until after his death. The volume was reissued by Losfeld in 1970, over Péret's name but still with its false title.

7. Benjamin Péret, *Anthologie de l'Amour sublime,* p. 72. This statement is misquoted as "The sacred is born of love," in Marie-Odile Blanquaert, "The Mythe de 'l'amour sublime' dans *Feu central* de Benjamin Péret," *Cahiers Dada surréalisme* 1 (1966), 65.

8. "Allo" is translated in its entirety in J. H. Matthews, trans., *Péret's Score / Vingt poèmes de Benjamin Péret* (Lettres Modernes, 1965), pp. 43 and 45.

Chapter Nine

1. Benjamin Péret, *Air mexicain* (Arcanes 1952). The date of composition is September, 1949.

2. Péret contributed his poem to a collective tribute, *Violette Nozières,* put out by the Surrealists after the trial and conviction of Violette Nozières for murdering her father, who had raped her (Brussels: Editions Nicolas Flamel, 1933).

3. André Breton, *Les Pas perdus,* p. 210.

4. Benjamin Péret, *La Parole est à Péret,* Pauvert edition, p. 54. *Anthologie des Mythes, légendes et contes populaires d'Amérique,* p. 25.

5. Benjamin Péret, *La Parole est à Péret,* pp. 54–55. *Anthologie des Mythes,* p. 25.

6. Chiappe closed the movie house where Buñuel's *L'Age d'Or* was showing. Buñuel was not to forget this when making his *Journal d'une femme de chambre.* For details see J. H. Matthews, *Surrealism and Film,* p. 105.

7. An *habitué* is an unbeneficed priest as well as an habitual visitor.

8. Benjamin Péret, Response published in *Le Peignoir de Bain,* no. 4, 1954, cited in Mayoux, "Benjamin Péret, la fourchette coupante," pt. 2, p. 54.

9. Benjamin Péret, "Du fond de la forêt," *Le Surréalisme, même,* no. 2 (Spring, 1957), 106.

10. For the benefit of readers unacquainted with the term "French letters," it should be pointed out that the French familiarly ascribe the invention and/or habitual use of the condom (named, after all, for an eighteenth-century English doctor, reputed to be its inventor) to the English. The compliment is returned from across the Chanel. Cf. "*filer à l'anglaise*" and "to take French leave."

Chapter Ten

1. Benjamin Péret, "Le Sang répandu," *Le Grand Jeu*, I, 182.
2. Quoted in Jehan Mayoux, "Benjamin Péret, la fourchette coupante," pt. 1, p. 156.

Selected Bibliography

PRIMARY SOURCES

Unless otherwise indicated, the place of publication for all books is Paris.

1921   *Le Passager du transatlantique.* Collection "Dada."
1923   *Au 125 du boulevard Saint-Germain.* Collection "Littérature."
1924   *Immortelle Maladie.* Collection "Littérature."
1925   *Il était une boulangère.* Aux Editions du Sagittaire, chez Simon Kra.
       152 Proverbes mis au goût du jour (in collaboration with Paul Eluard). Editions surréalistes.
1927   *Dormir, dormir dans les pierres.* Editions surréalistes.
       Au Grand Jour (in collaboration with Louis Aragon, André Breton, Paul Eluard, and Pierre Unik). Editions surréalistes.
1928   *... Et les Seins mouraient....* Marseilles: Les Cahiers du Sud.
       Le Grand Jeu. Gallimard.
1929   *1929* (in collaboration with Louis Aragon and Man Ray). No publisher.
1934   *De Derrière les fagots.* Editions surréalistes, chez J. Corti.
1936   *Je ne mange pas de ce pain-là.* Editions surréalistes.
       Je sublime. Editions suréalistes.
       Trois Cerises et une sardine. Editions G.L.M.
1938   *Au Paradis des fantômes.* Collection "Un Divertissement."
1942   *Les Malheurs d'un dollar.* Editions de la Main à Plume.
1943   *La Parole est à Péret.* New York, Editions surréalistes.
1945   *Le Déshonneur des poètes.* Mexico City, Poésie et Révolution.
       Dernier Malheur, dernière chance. Editions de la revue *Fontaine.*
1946   *Main forte.* Editions de la revue *Fontaine.*
1947   *Feu central.* Editions K.
1949   *La Brebis galante.* Les Editions premières.
1952   *Air mexicain.* Librairie Arcanes.
1953   *Mort aux Vaches et au champ d'honneur.* Editions Arcanes.
       Toyen (in collaboration with André Breton and Jindrich Heisler). Editions Sokolova.

1954   *Les Rouilles encagées* (*Les Couilles enragées*). Eric Losfeld
        (published under the pseudonym Satyremont).
1955   *Livre de Chilám Balám de Chumayel.* Denoël.
1956   *Anthologie de l'Amour sublime.* Editions Albin Michel.
1957   *Le Gigot, sa vie et son œuvre.* Le Terrain Vague.
1958   *Histoire naturelle.* Ussel: privately printed.
        La poesia surrealista francese. Milan: Schwarz.
1960   *Anthologie des Mythes, légendes et contes populaires
        d'Amérique.* Editions Albin Michel.
1963   *Dames et Généraux.* Milan: Schwarz; Paris: Berggruen.
1965   *Pour un Second Manifeste Communiste* (in collaboration with
        G. Munis). Le Terrain Vague.
1968   *Les Mains dans les poches.* Montpellier: Léo éditeur.
        Les Syndicats contre la Révolution (in collaboration with G.
        Munis). Le Terrain Vague.
1969   *Œuvres complètes,* vol. I. Eric Losfeld.
1971   *Œuvres complètes,* vol. II. Eric Losfeld.

ENGLISH TRANSLATIONS

1. Essays

"Magic: The Flesh and Blood of Poetry" (abridged translation of
    La Parole est à Péret). *View,* series 3, no. 2, 1943. Reprinted in
    Antinarcissus: Surrealist Conquest 1 (Summer, 1969), 3–9, 30.
"Thought is ONE and indivisible." *Free Union libres,* 1946, 3–4.
    Reprinted in *Surrealism and Revolution.* Chicago: Solidarity,
    1966.
"Notes on Pre-Columbian Art." *Horizon,* vol. 15, no. 89, 1947.
"Remembrance of Things to Come." *Trans/formation* 1 (1952),
    173–75.
"The Dishonor of Poets." *Radical America* 4, no. 6 (August, 1970),
    15–20.
"The Factory Committee: Motor of the Social Revolution." *Radical
    America* 4, no. 6 (August, 1970), 21–23.
"Poetry above all." *Radical America* 4, no. 6 (August, 1970), 23–24.

2. Stories

"At 125, Boulevard Saint-Germain." *This Quarter,* Surrealist num-
    ber, 1932.
"In a Clinch." *transition,* 12. Reprinted in *transition Workshop.* New
    York: Vanguard Press, 1949.

"The Thaw." *VVV* 1 (June, 1942), 14–16. Reprinted in the "Surrealist Section" of the anthology *New Road*, Billericky, Essex: The Grey Walls Press, 1943, and in *Radical America* 4, no. 6 (August, 1970), 25–27.
The Gallant Sheep, chapter 4. *Radical America*, Special issue: "Surrealism in the Service of the Revolution" (January, 1970), 39.

3. Poems

A Bunch of Carrots. Trans. Humphrey Jennings, David Gascoyne, *et al.* London: Contemporary Poetry and Prose Editions, 1936.
Remove Your Hat. Trans. Humphrey Jennings, David Gascoyne, *et al.* London: Contemporary Poetry and Prose Editions, 1936.
Péret's Score / Vingt poèmes de Benjamin Péret. Trans. J. H. Matthews. Lettres Modernes, 1965, Collection "Passeport," no. 10.
Individual poems by Péret have appeared in *Arsenal: Surrealist Subversion; Contemporary Poetry and Prose; London Bulletin; New Directions; Radical America; Rebel Worker; This Quarter; View;* and Julien Levy, *Surrealism,* New York: The Black Sun Press, 1936.

SECONDARY SOURCES

With the exception of the last, all the authors of the works listed below participated in the Surrealist movement. Works cited are arranged in chronological order.

NAVILLE, PIERRE. "Benjamin Péret." *La Revue européene,* no. 26, April 1, 1925; reproduced in Benjamin Péret, *Œuvres complètes,* volume II. An essay on the "purity" of Benjamin Péret, by the man who coedited with him the first issues of *La Révolution surréaliste.*
ELUARD, PAUL. "L'Arbitraire, la contradiction, la violence, la poésie." *Variétés,* June 15, 1929. An interesting militant essay on Péret's poetry by a man whose poems differ radically from Péret's. An edited version of this text appears in Eluard's *Donner à voir* (1939) where, suppressing all references to Péret, Eluard offers remarks originally inspired by Péret's writings as a commentary on poetry in general. The text in *Donner à voir* reproduces an edited version of Eluard's lecture "L'Evidence poétique," delivered in London on June 24, 1936, in the context of the London International Surrealist Exhibition.
BRETON, ANDRÉ. "Benjamin Péret." In his *Anthologie de l'Humour noir* (1940), definitive edition published by J. J. Pauvert, 1966,

pp. 505–7; reproduced in Benjamin Péret, *Œuvres complètes,* volume I. On Péret's revolutionary use of language.

MAYOUX, JEHAN. "Benjamin Péret, la fourchette coupante." *Le Surréalisme, même,* no. 2 (Spring, 1957), 151–58 and no. 3 (Autumn, 1957), 53–58. The first relatively extended study of Péret, as poet and anticlerical sociopolitical revolutionary.

BÉDOUIN, JEAN-LOUIS. "Présentation" (pp. 9–74). In *Benjamin Péret* (Pierre Seghers, 1961), "Poètes d'aujourd'hui" series, no. 78. An extensive essay by a fellow Surrealist in whose home Péret found refuge toward the end of his life.

COURTOT, CLAUDE. *Introduction à la lecture de Benjamin Péret.* Le Terrain Vague, 1966. Sponsored by the Association of the Friends of Benjamin Péret, founded in May, 1963, this study by a young acolyte who aggressively, but not very convincingly, adopts the Surrealist posture, does not fulfill its stated purpose, that of establishing Péret's originality and according him the place he deserves.

SCHUSTER, JEAN. "Péret de profil." Reprinted in Schuster's *Archives 57/68: batailles pour le surréalisme.* Losfeld, 1969. This pretentious essay was written originally to introduce the reprint *Le Déshonneur des poètes* précédé de *La Parole est à Péret* (J. J. Pauvert, 1965).

BENAYOUN, ROBERT. "A plus d'un titre. . . ." Preface to a reprint of *Le Grand Jeu.* Gallimard, 1969, Collection "Poésie." Pertinent and informative on Péret as poet.

ROSEMONT, FRANKLIN. "An Introduction to Benjamin Péret." *Radical America* 4, no. 6 (August, 1970), 1–13. A militant article on Péret as revolutionary, intended for the American public, by an American Surrealist.

BAILLY, JEAN-CHRISTOPHE. *"Au-delà du langage": Une étude sur Benjamin Péret.* Eric Losfeld, 1971. Touches on some important aspects of Péret's poetic language, though it does not examine them closely enough.

Index

173